MINDFULNESS
MADE EASY

MINDFULNESS MADE EASY

50 simple practices to reduce stress,
create calm, and live in the moment
—at home, work and school

Maureen F. Fitzgerald, PhD

CENTERPOINT MEDIA

CenterPoint Media
www.CenterPointInc.com

LIBRARY AND ARCHIVES CANADA CATALOGUING IN PUBLICATION

Fitzgerald, Maureen F., author
        Mindfulness made easy : 50 simple practices to reduce stress, create calm and live in the moment -at home, work and school / Maureen F. Fitzgerald, PHD.

Includes bibliographical references.
Issued in print and electronic formats.

ISBN 978-0-9939840-3-7 (paperback)
ISBN 978-1-988072-03-6 (ebook)

1. Self-realization. 2. Calmness. 3. Stress management.
4. Mindfulness (Psychology). I. Title.

BF637.S4F577 2015   158.1   C2015-905612-8
                                           C2015-905613-6

Layout and design: Maureen Cutajar, Go Published
Cover design: Christine Unterthiner, Pilot Brand
Cover image: Getty Images
Author photo: www.phototobinphotography.com
Editing: Paper Trail Publishing

Reprinted with permission: Coleman Barks: *The Guest House* by Jalaluddin Rumi; excerpt from *The Prophet* by Kahlil Gibran, c.1923; Knopf, Penguin Random House.

To all my meditation teachers including my family,
for opening my mind and my heart

Contents

Introduction 1

Chapter 1   Your Body 9

1   Notice your breath 11
2   Do a body scan 13
3   Use all of your senses...........................15
4   Eat mindfully 17
5   Be totally present 19
6   Smell mindfully 21
7   Walk mindfully 23
8   Listen to your body 25
9   Go very slowly 27
10   Practice yoga...29

Chapter 2   Your Mind 33

11   Adopt a beginner's mind.....................35
12   Notice your monkey mind 37
13   Live in the now 39
14   Meditate 42
15   Feel gratitude 45
16   Practice affirmations........................... 47
17   Visualize 49
18   Avoid assumptions 51
19   Find your passion..................................53
20   Stop for a sacred pause 55

Chapter 3   Your Heart 57

21   Notice your feelings..............................59
22   Pay attention to stress 61

23 Attend to your pain.. 63

24 Listen to your sadness 65

25 Befriend yourself.. 67

26 Go on a media diet 69

27 Practice loving-kindness 71

28 Notice the judge 73

29 Accept the good and the bad 75

30 Try compassion 77

Chapter 4   Your World 79

31 Listen and be heard... 81

32 Speak mindfully 83

33 Clarify your intentions 86

34 Suspend judgment 88

35 Apologize and forgive 90

36 Celebrate mistakes 93

37 Avoid perfectionism 95

38 Practice optimism... 97

39 Notice your triggers 100

40 Question productivity and time............................ 102

Chapter 5   Your Life.. 105

41 Do mindful art... 107

42 Try a labyrinth or mandala 109

43 Create a sacred space 111

44 Dance 113

45 Never judge a book by its cover........................... 115

46 Live life with joy.. 117

47 Embrace all of life 120

48 Feast on life 122

49 Accept your journey 124

50 Accept yourself completely................................... 126

Conclusion.. 129

Resources 131

About the Author... 135

Teachers open the door, but you must enter by yourself.
—Chinese proverb

Introduction

*Simply put, mindfulness is moment-to-moment awareness. It is
cultivated by purposely paying attention to things we ordinarily
never give a moment's thought to.*
—Jon Kabat-Zinn, *Full Catastrophe Living*

After ten years of practicing mindfulness, I am convinced that if you practice regularly, you will not only be able to better deal with life's stresses, but you will also become a better person. You will feel more alive, more joyful and even more productive. You will be able to truly smell the roses, no matter how busy you are.

I want to do only one thing with this book: I want to give you a taste of what mindfulness is so you want to do it more and more. I don't want you to wait to experience the benefits of mindfulness until you have turned fifty, read thirty books on the topic or attended several workshops or retreats (like I have). I wish to make mindfulness practices accessible, among others, to teachers, counselors, parents and lawyers, to both young and old, so they can experience its many benefits.

My story

A few years ago I had a wake-up call while attending a talk on stress and anxiety at my teenage daughters' school. I was greeted with shocking statistics showing that anxiety disorders and depression are impacting record numbers of teenagers. In one local school, eight teenagers had attempted suicide in the previous year. This information hit me particularly hard, having just completed my doctoral research and having found the same problem among lawyers, doctors and other professionals. Could it be that stress is not a personal problem and that we are all suffering in ways never seen in prior generations?

Anxiety is an epidemic

According to recent research, anxiety is the number one mental health problem in North America today. Many of us move constantly at breakneck speed under enormous strains, pressures and expectations. As a result, we are frenzied, frayed, disconnected, and filled with anxious thoughts. We rarely allow ourselves to slow down.

Worse yet, most people suffer with their anxiety alone in silence. Only a few seek therapy and learn a handful of coping strategies. Others obtain anxiety medications or are urged to exercise and eat better. But those who seek help are few and the therapies can be costly, to individuals, families and workplace.

Research shows mindfulness works

Yet the newest research on anxiety shows that mindfulness-based therapy is completely shifting the way psychologists and counselors look at the human condition and our responses to life pressures. The research reveals that mindfulness helps people deal with both physical and emotional pain, stress, anxiety, depression and attention deficit/hyperactivity disorder (ADHD). And this research began more than thirty-five years ago.

In 1979, Jon Kabat-Zinn, a molecular biologist, founded the now-popular Mindfulness-Based Stress Reduction (MBSR) program at the University of Massachusetts Medical Center. His early research on anxiety and chronic pain showed significant reduction in stress.

That rigorously tested program is now being taught at over 250 hospitals across the United States.

In addition, physicians such as Dr. Daniel Siegel have developed cutting-edge therapies such as Mindfulness-Based Cognitive Therapy (MBCT), which is being used extensively by psychologists and counselors across North America.

Adding to this research on mindfulness is the data gathered by teachers about social and emotional learning (SEL) and its profound impact on learning, thinking and emotional intelligence. In recent years the Hawn Foundation, established by the actor Goldie Hawn, introduced the successful MindUP program to hundreds of schools in the United States and Canada, a program based in neuroscience, positive psychology and mindful awareness training. In other parts of the world, scholars and sages continue to refine ancient philosophies and practices, such as Buddhism, making them more accessible to the general public. Pema Chödrön, Sharon Salzberg and Jack Kornfield are such leaders, and their books are well worth reading.

But to the general population, mindfulness is still somewhat foreign and few people know about the powerful impact it can have on stress, anxiety and everyday life. Although it has found its way into hospitals and therapists' offices, it is almost non-existent in workplaces.

I wrote this book not to tell you about all the amazing research in this field, but rather to give you a quick and practical introduction to mindfulness so you can experience it for yourself.

Here is the secret

Even after ten years of practice, I still find it difficult to sit still and meditate. Luckily, I now know you do not need to sit on a pillow in order to become more relaxed, calm and focused. The secret is to commit to trying your best to stay completely awake to all that is happening. This means staying in the present moment, here and now. Although learning this skill is quite easy, making it a habit is not so simple. In fact, being mindful is often more about *unlearning our bad habits,* like rushing, panicking and clinging, and replacing them with new habits, like accepting and loving.

Frequently asked questions

Before reading the practices described in this book, it's useful to know a bit about mindfulness. Here are answers to some frequently asked questions.

What is mindfulness?
Mindfulness means being fully aware or awake. It means being aware of your body, of your thoughts, of your senses and all of your experiences. It also means being awake to your reactions, your emotions and the impact you have on those around you. Mindfulness is about *paying attention on purpose* in a friendly, nonjudgmental way, so you can experience life more fully. Through mindfulness you get in touch with your body, pay attention to your "monkey mind," and reconnect with your emotions and with those of others.

The mindful approach to stress and anxiety is to understand what is happening and then approach it with a new perspective. It is about being conscious of what is happening within your body and mind and noticing how your thoughts and emotions are controlling you.

Mindfulness is not about being right or wrong; it's about practicing techniques that will allow you to see yourself and your world more clearly, so you can respond more appropriately. It's about admitting that everyone experiences difficulties (not just you) and everyone can learn by being mindful of how to relate and respond to those troubles.

What are mindful practices?
Mindful practices include both formal and informal techniques to help you to be more aware. From meditating on a cushion to day-to-day practices, each of the practices in this book is designed to help you be more awake to what is here right now, in the moment. Through mindfulness practices, you become attuned to your body, thoughts,

emotions and all of your life experiences so you can better use this information to embrace life and live with more ease. By being mindful, you can reduce stress, but more importantly, you can develop powerful habits and healthier ways of thinking, feeling and responding.

Where did the practices come from?

Mindfulness practices are rooted in 2,500-year-old meditative and contemplative traditions. Although originally only permitted to be practiced by a chosen few, these practices are now available to all, regardless of religion. For many years and all around the world, researchers, doctors, therapists, teachers, nurses and educators have been developing and testing the effectiveness of hundreds of different mindfulness practices.

Isn't mindfulness a Buddhist practice?

Mindful practices are not related to any formal religion, although many are based on ancient Buddhist meditation practices. Most formal religions embrace these contemplative practices, particularly silence, prayer and meditation. Many modern body-based practices also involve mindfulness, such as yoga, tai chi and qigong.

What are the benefits of mindfulness?

Research shows that mindfulness has significant benefits, including the following:
- Mindfulness reduces anxiety, creates a state of calm and builds resilience.
- Mindfulness enhances the ability to concentrate and focus.
- Mindfulness makes us feel more alive and more empathetic.
- Mindfulness promotes acceptance, less judging and more open-mindedness.

Over time, mindfulness can create positive states of mind that allow greater insight into and understanding of ourselves and the world around us.

Isn't mindfulness just meditation, relaxation or zoning out?

Mindfulness-based meditation does involve sitting still and being silent, but it does not equate with zoning out. Indeed, it entails the opposite. Although your body is relaxed during mindfulness practices, you are directly relating to all of your experiences. You are not running away from your problems or sitting in a trance.

Unlike basic relaxation techniques, mindfulness heightens your awareness of the present moment and encourages you to embrace—not avoid—all of your experiences, whether positive or negative , moment by moment.

How does mindfulness work?

In Western culture we tend to think of anxiety and stress as a disease or something that needs to be cured. We are told that anxiety is a personal problem, that it is temporary and that it will often go away. We believe we simply need to be stronger to be able to cope with day-to-day stresses. , we take pills and drink alcohol, and we read books about how we can be tougher, more tolerant, not so sensitive to "normal" difficulties.

If you visit a Western-trained counselor, you will likely be urged to deal with your stress in three overlapping ways. You will probably be told that you need to *think differently* and could benefit from cognitive behavioral therapy (CBT) or by replacing your problematic thoughts with better ones. You might be told that your emotions are out of proportion and you could learn to *feel differently* by learning body relaxation and mind control techniques. Finally, you might be told to *behave differently* by learning how to control your physical or verbal responses.

Under this Western ideology, people experiencing anxiety and stress are told there is something wrong with them and then told what they need to do to "get better." In other words, if you are suffering, you are told not only that you are the problem, but also that you must change—often immediately. Although it sounds strange, you are told that you are not good enough just as you are.

But the truth is that anxiety and stress are by-products of living in this world. They are human conditions that never really go away. We all experience illness, aging, death and uncertainty. They are unavoidable facts of life. We all suffer stress from these events to some degree;

the only difference is how wisely we respond. In other words, do we freak out, panic and have knee-jerk reactions, or do we approach difficulties with mindfulness, wisdom and a sense of calm?

Mindfulness is not about telling you how to change or to be better. It is about acknowledging and being open to all that is happening. It is about noticing, observing and accepting yourself completely so you are able to eventually respond in ways that are more skillful.

How to use this book

Each of the fifty practices is easy and fun. Each introduces a creative way to explore and experiment with a fresh way of being in your life. As you try out these practices, you will feel more at ease and alive, you will feel calmer and at peace, and you will enjoy more compassionate relationships.

Here are some general guidelines when using this book.

- Each practice is a separate exercise designed to enhance your ability to be mindful.
- Each practice should take only a few minutes, but many can last longer if you wish.
- You can select any practice in any order, although the body practices tend to be the easiest.
- You can do one or more practices in a sitting.
- Feel free to tailor the practices so they are truly your own.

These practices are not things to be added to your chores list and should only be done when your curiosity is piqued. Most of all, you cannot do any of them "wrong." There are no mistakes. They are just practices. You may want to do them over and over and may find that each time something else shows up.

If you like this book—next steps

If you enjoy this book and are keen to be even more mindful, I would suggest the following three strategies: read lots of books in mindfulness and meditation, watch online videos, and listen to podcasts and audios. For some suggestions, check out the list of resources at the end of this book. I love reading Pema Chödrön's books over and over. You might also enjoy taking a basic course in mindfulness meditation, like MBSR, or join a regular sitting or study group.

I sit with a group once a week, which is lovely, and I attend retreats and lectures whenever I can. Life is hard and it requires practice to respond in an enlightened and skillful way. The most important step is the commitment to continually work at becoming more skillful, admitting you are not as skilled as you might like, but that you will keep trying. Whatever you do, do not let your friends or your ego tell you that all of this is a waste of time. Changing ingrained habits is difficult, and being mindful will at times feel like a bit of a drag, but you can do it, and the practices are most definitely worthwhile.

I feel honoured and blessed to be able to travel in the footsteps of masters including Jack Kornfield, Tara Brach, Jon Kabat-Zinn, Daniel Siegel, Pema Chödrön, Mark Epstein, Ellen Langer, Thích Nhất Hạnh, Amy Salzman , Sharon Salzberg and Joseph Goldstein, Bob Stahl and so many more.

Although life seems to be zooming by, the real richness of life becomes available when you are present for it. The more you pay attention to what is happening here and now, the more you can enjoy life and not dwell on the future or the past. When you are being present, you feel a sense of peace and ease. You relax and release stress. You don't have to stop what you are doing. You just have to mentally shift and say, "I am here. I am mindful."

Chapter 1

Your Body

Notice your breath

*The act of breathing is one of the most fundamental processes
of life itself. In many sacred traditions, the breath is recognized
as the sources of vital energy for both body and mind.*
—Cathy Malchiodi, *The Soul's Palette*

What it is. When we get anxious, we tend to fall into the habit of
shallow, rapid breathing. This results in more tension in our bodies
and sends less oxygen to the lungs. Because breathing is automatic,
we take it for granted. We do not realize that we may be breathing
quickly or slowly, shallowly or deeply—or breathing at all. Yet research shows that deep breathing can not only slow your
metabolism and lower your body temperature, but also slow your
heart rate and even create altered states and healing. Indeed, it has
been shown that seven deep breaths can both clear and calm your
brain. Deep breathing, however, requires conscious effort—beyond
our natural impulse. This practice will help you become aware of
your breath and be better able to use your breath to induce calm.

How to do it. You need from 5 to 15 minutes for this practice. Find a
quiet place where you can be alone for a short while. Sit in a chair
with your feet flat on the floor. Settle in until you feel stable, and
breathe normally. After a few breaths, relax. Now take several quick
breaths in and out, as if you were running or were pumping your

lungs. After a few rapid breaths, relax. Then take a few very deep breaths and slow your breathing as much as you can. After a few long, slow breaths, relax. Return to your regular breathing. Finally, take one really deep breath and try to pull the air deep into your stomach, as if you were inflating an air mattress.

If you find your breath is shallow, try to breathe deep into your diaphragm (the muscle between your chest and your abdomen). Imagine cool air moving in and warm air moving out. If your chest is rising more than your belly, try to reverse this, sending more air into your belly. Keep in mind, however, that mindful breathing is not so much about controlling your breath as it is about noticing it.

What to notice. Can you feel the air moving in through your nose and mouth and into your lungs? Can you feel it circulating in your body? Notice how the air actually lifts you up and then gently down, into a settled state. Do you notice that simply breathing causes your shoulders to drop? When you are consciously breathing, are you less or more aware of what is going on around you?

Practice 2

Do a body scan

Learn to be calm and you will always be happy.
—Paramahansa Yogananda

What it is. The body scan is a fundamental practice of mindfulness. It is a way to monitor what is going on at a physical level and also a way to relax the body, bit by bit. Also called muscle relaxation, this practice was refined by the American physician Edmund Jacobson in the 1930s. It is often used to activate the body upon waking and to slow down the body before sleeping.

The body scan involves either sitting or lying down with your eyes closed and mentally scanning your body from head to toe and back again. Rather than using your eyes, you use your senses to listen to each of your body parts.

How to do it. You need about 10 minutes for this practice. Lie down on your back and breathe deeply in and out three times. Prepare to both contract and relax every muscle group in your body. Starting with your toes, tense them for five seconds and then release them. Next, tense your arches, then your calf muscles, and so on. Move up your body to your torso and limbs, and all the way up to your neck, face and scalp. Try to become aware of where you are holding tension and practice actively letting go of it wherever you find it. Breathe deeply throughout and if you wish, breathe into each muscle as you relax.

What to notice. Do you notice any areas of tightness, tension or pain? Do you feel a tickling sensation or release when you focus on a particular area of your body? Some people feel energy emanating through the body. At the end of the scan, you should experience a restful awareness of your whole body and may even sense the energy field around your body.

Practice 3

Use all of your senses

You can bring mindful presence into doing the laundry, washing dishes or making dinner. These small routine ceremonies are opportunities to still your mind and give you a small breathing space within the hurly-burly of everyday life.
—Jeffrey Brantley and Wendy Millstine, *Five Good Minutes*

What it is. Although all humans have five senses—sight, taste, touch, smell and hearing—we tend to favor one or two, causing the others to sit relatively dormant. This practice will help you activate all of your senses.

How to do it. For this exercise you need a group of at least five (and up to thirty) people and a bag of navel oranges. When everyone is sitting, ask each person to take one orange from the bag. Have each person touch their orange, smell the orange and look at it closely. Ask them to note any particular markings on the orange, since they will be asked to identify it later. After about three minutes, have each person place the orange back in the bag. Mix them around and then pour the oranges into a pile in the middle of the room. Finally, ask each person to come up and select their orange.

What to notice. It is surprising when each person identifies their own orange. Often we assume oranges are all the same and we don't

take the time to see how unique each one is. By being more atten-
tive, you begin to notice the subtle differences in everything—from
fruit to the weather and particularly in people you do not know well.
You wake up to the realization that every single thing and every moment is different and that mindfully using your senses is a powerful
tool of observation and understanding.

Practice 4

Eat mindfully

Since preparing and eating food is such an essential component
of our lives, why not bring mindful awareness to this?
—Bob Stahl and Elisha Goldstein, *A Mindfulness-Based Stress*
Reduction Workbook

What it is. The speed at which we eat in Western society is shocking. Some meals at my own house are finished in less than 10 minutes. Not only is eating quickly bad for digestion, but when we eat speedily, we barely taste what we eat or savor our food. We miss out on the simple pleasure of eating, as well as the information emanating from our body as we chew and swallow. We don't notice our taste buds reacting, our throat constricting or our stomach digesting. And when we're done, we don't know whether we are full or still hungry.

In the popular MindUP program created by actor Goldie Hawn, elementary school students are asked to use words to describe the various tastes they sense when they are eating. They describe foods as bitter, salty, sweet, sour, tangy, lemony, bland or sharp. When they use the descriptive words, not only do students slow down their eating, but they also become more selective and more conscious eaters.

How to do it. Place a raisin in your hand. Look closely at the raisin and notice its shape, color and texture. Smell the raisin. Take your time. Now place the raisin on your tongue. Do not bite it right way. Just roll it around in your mouth and feels its bumps and contours. Notice that your mouth is salivating. Notice the urge to bite and swallow. Slowly bite down into the raisin and feel your teeth and jaw pressing down. Notice the burst of taste in your mouth and where on your tongue the taste is registering. Roll the raisin to the back of your tongue and swallow. Sense it going down your esophagus. Breathe deeply and reflect on how the experience felt.

What to notice. How is eating in this way different than how you eat on a regular basis? After doing this practice, most people say it's the first time they've really tasted a raisin. Also, when engaged in this way, you might notice that your mind does not wander elsewhere. You have the pleasure of doing only one thing with complete attention, free from other distracting thoughts.

Practice 5

Be totally present

[People] measure their esteem of each other by what each has, and not by what each is.... Nothing can bring you peace but yourself.
—Ralph Waldo Emerson

What it is. You may have heard of the concept of "living in the now" or being present. This means trying to live right here, right now without looking ahead or looking back. It means being totally alert and awake to all that is going on, both inside you and around you. Sad to say, we rarely live in the present. We rarely stop to smell the roses. We all tend to worry too much about what may happen in the future or stress about what has happened in the past.

The skill of being fully alert and centered is best seen in those who practice martial arts. They are trained to be so calm on the inside that they can respond appropriately to any attack. Like a well-rooted tree, they are completely here in the present moment and as a result can weather even violent storms.

How to do it. Next time you do a simple chore like sweeping the floor or washing dishes, take the opportunity to do the task mindfully. Instead of thinking of other things or daydreaming, fully focus on what you are doing with complete curiosity and calm. Feel the handle of the broom in your hands. Watch the shape of the bristles as they press against the floor. Notice the dirt flecks as they move into the dustpan. If you are washing dishes, feel the temperature of the dishwater. Smell the soap suds. Become fully absorbed in the moment and sense how freeing it feels to be fully engaged in the present. Another easy way to be more in the present is to mix up your habits. For example, walk to work a different way or eat a different breakfast or sit in a place that's new for you.

What to notice. When you focus on the present moment, it is as if all of your senses come alive. You see things you have never noticed before. All the mental energy that might have been spread over many things is now focused on just one thing: being here now. This feels similar to moving from multitasking to working on only one project. Your levels of concentration and observation increase significantly. All the other distractions fall away. As you go about your day, try to notice how often you are truly in the present moment.

Practice 6

Smell mindfully

Mindfulness, bravery and compassion and wisdom are not born overnight but nor are they remote and unattainable qualities. They can be awakened, and once awakened, will inspire others.
—Jane Hope, *The Meditation Year*

What it is. Mindful smelling involves noticing when your sense of smell is being activated and understanding its impact on you. Our sense of smell is our most powerful sense. For some, the smell of freshly baked bread, clean sheets or popcorn can evoke a sense of comfort. For others, the smell of a mother's perfume can stimulate forgotten memories. The smell of smoke or gas can alert us to danger. The smell of food cooking can remind us that we are hungry. Without a sense of smell, we cannot taste! Unfortunately, many of us do not even realize when our noses are stimulated or the impact that smells have on our entire sense of well-being. We often only notice a smell when it's extreme, like when the oven is on fire or there is mold on our yogurt.

How to do it. With another person, go to your kitchen and open up a food or spice cupboard. Select a few items that have distinct smells, like lemongrass, peanut butter, coffee or vinegar. Take turns closing your eyes while the other person moves items under your nose. Guess what the item is and reflect on whether it brings back a memory or feeling.

What to notice. How is mindful smelling different than the smelling you do automatically, day in and day out? How many smells do you notice in an average day? If you slowed down, do you think you would notice more smells? Do some smells make you calmer or more agitated? Although we can all smell with our noses, it comes as a surprise to most that we do not use our noses as much as we could. It's as if we need to retrain ourselves to smell again. We have all heard the phrase "Stop and smell the roses," but for most of us it seems so difficult to notice all the wonder and beauty that sur- rounds us unless we stop or at least slow down.

Practice 7

Walk mindfully

What we really seek is not the surface goals [like money and status] are just means to an end. What we are really after is the feeling of relief that comes when the drive is satisfied. Relief, relaxation, and an end to the tension. Peace happiness—no more yearning.
—Bhante Gunaratana, *Mindfulness in Plain English*

What it is. Not long ago I attended a one-hour mindful practice with a group of lawyers. We were led through a practice of mindful walking but were limited because the room had a huge oblong table in the middle. As a result, we eight lawyers found ourselves marching at a rigorous speed around the outside of the table. Needless to say, this was not helpful for getting centered, but it did remind me how quickly we can revert back to old habits, particularly when we are following the pace of those in front of us.

Some beginners to meditation find sitting difficult so prefer to walk when trying to be mindful. Although moving your body in meditation can help with focus, there is a danger of falling into a trance and walking too quickly, often on automatic pilot. Because we feel rushed most days, we rarely even notice the speed at which we are walking. We rush to the bathroom, we run to the elevator, we scurry to catch the bus or a taxi. We rarely slow our pace. Walking mindfully can help us to slow down.

How to do it. Pick a quiet location inside or outside where you can walk for at least ten paces without interruption. Stand still and center yourself. Take a few deep breaths. Sense the air and space around you, and notice your hands and feet and body. Stand up tall and align your body so you feel like a string is pulling you up through your head. Focus your eyes slightly downward and ahead of where you will be walking. Ever so slowly begin to walk, sensing first the lifting of the leg and the placing of the foot. Sense the shift of balance and feel the ground. Relax your body and mind. Notice how you shift your weight from one foot to the other to test your balance. As you step, notice how your foot strikes the ground, heel to toe. Notice how your arms and torso move. Walk as slowly as possible without losing balance. Be aware of the ground under your feet and the sound of your steps.

What to notice. At first you may feel stiff, awkward and off-balance. Slowly you will get into a gentle rhythm or pace and will eventually synchronize your steps with your breathing. As you walk, your thoughts and emotions will arise. As they do, try again to focus on your body moving and your steps. In doing so, your thoughts may begin to float away with each step. Slowly. The point of walking meditation is to become more aware of your walking, as well as to use your walking as a focus to keep distractions at bay. Additionally, the natural movement of each step will cultivate your overall mindfulness. You will become more aware, alert, centered and calm.

Practice 8

Listen to your body

The moment one gives close attention to anything, even a blade of grass, it becomes a mysterious, awesome, indescribably magnificent world in itself.
—Henry Miller

What it is. We are often so busy in our minds that we completely forget about our bodies. Mindfulness expert and author Tara Brach suggests returning to your body as often as you can each day. When you do, you'll see how your body is continually taking in and giving out vibrations and energy. As children, we rarely learn how to really listen to the messages from our body or how to understand them. Mindful listening begins with simply noticing when your body tenses or relaxes in response to your emotions—such as when you feel angry, pressured or criticized, or when you are excited or calm. It also involves watching how you respond to these sensations and emotions and understanding their impact on you.

How to do it. Sit in complete silence for a few moments. Take three deep breaths. Do you feel any tension in your body? Is your neck stiff? Are your legs comfortable? Is your nose itchy? Does your skin feel warm or cool? Can you hear your heart pumping, your stomach growling? Now think about your feet. What do they feel like? Wiggle your toes. Flex your foot from side to side. Rotate your ankle. Press the ball of your foot against the ground. Now let it flop. How do your feet feel now? You can focus on and activate any part of your body, such as your hands or arms. Often if you simply relax your shoulders, jaw and belly, you can activate an overall sense of well-being in your body.

What to notice. If you listen closely to your body's sensations, you may hear hundreds of tiny little messages. Over time you may begin to understand what they might be saying, messages like "Get more sleep," or "You are thirsty, not hungry!" They might be trying to alert you to something like danger or urging you to open your heart in forgiveness. Some agitation is a sign that you need to wait before making a decision, whereas other agitation is a sign you need to act immediately.

Once you notice your sensations and their impact, you can better understand why your body is behaving this way and you can make the necessary adjustments. If you're feeling stressed, for example, you may know the feeling has to do with a comment someone made about your work or with not getting a full night's sleep. You can choose to send energy directly to those bodily areas that are seizing up, you can choose to take some downtime, or you can choose to push your emotions away for the time being. With increased mindfulness, you can select the most appropriate response given your circumstances at that particular moment.

Practice 9

Go very slowly

Not causing harm requires staying awake. Part of being awake
is slowing down enough to notice what we say and do. The
more we witness our emotional chain reactions and understand
how they work, it's easier to refrain. It becomes a way of life to
stay awake, slow down and notice.
—Pema Chödrön, *Start Where You Are*

What it is. You may have heard of the internationally successful slow food movement. It was started by a handful of people who believe that we should not rush food. We should not rush growing food, harvesting food, preparing food and eating food. They wanted to reclaim the natural cycles of food and help humans get more in touch with the nourishment that keeps us alive. They have taught us how to savor food and relationships. What a great idea! Now there is even a slow medicine movement, combating the speed at which we diagnose and resolve medical issues.

As mentioned we in the West live our lives in a complete rush. We move from catastrophe to catastrophe in continual movement—seeing, responding, reacting, planning, eating, yelling and rarely pausing. We launch into situations and, before we know it, we are flipping out and blaming others for their foul moods, bad tempers or inappropriate responses. In reality, much of this reactiveness could be prevented if we simply slowed down a bit, giving ourselves time to pause before moving from one situation to the next.

How to do it. Think back over your first waking hour this morning. Recall in as much detail as possible what you did and whom you spoke to. Did you wake slowly and eat your breakfast calmly? Did you leap out of bed, rush into the shower and shovel down your breakfast—or skip it altogether? For the next hour, try to go as slowly as you possibly can. Notice your internal urge to pick up speed and where you feel it in your body. If you catch yourself rushing, simply stop, take three deep breaths, drop your shoulders, smile and continue.

The key to slowing down is mostly to notice how you are moving. When are you moving at breakneck speeds? When are you calm and in the flow? When are you completely still? Over time and with some reflection, you may begin to understand the deeper reasons for your compulsion to speed.

What to notice. The most obvious benefit to slowing down is the sense of relaxation you experience. It feels as if a weight has been lifted off your shoulders. Slowing down also causes your mind to clear. It's as though the fog lifts, if only for a second. You will be able to observe things that moments before were just a blur. Over time you may discover there is a little voice in your brain (I call it the slave driver telling you to never stop. This voice may be telling you things like "If you stop, you will be worthless or broke," or "No one likes lazy people." Being mindful of this voice (also called the ego) helps you understand the cultural or familial conditioning that makes it so hard for you to slow down.

Practice 10

Practice yoga

*Meditation relaxes the body, brings clarity and steadiness of
mind, and opens the heart.*
—Jane Hope, *The Meditation Year*

What it is. You may have tried yoga or other body-based practices
like Nia, tai chi or qigong. What you may not know is the importance of these practices to your state of mind and sense of well-
being. Growing up, many of us learned about the importance of getting exercise not truly knowing how these various exercises work
and how they impact everything we do.

Although most people know yoga and other movements as stretch-
ing regimes or sets of exercises, many are based on thousand-year-old
practices and are designed to move your body in such a way that energy
(also called chi) is able to move more freely. You not only loosen up
muscles and strengthen joints, but also activate the chakras or energy
points so you actually feel an energetic boost. By moving your bodies in
these fluid ways, you activate your body and your mind as well.

Your body consists of hundreds of muscles continually expanding and contracting—from the tip of your head to the bottom of
your feet. The more you move, the more these muscles and joints
stay alive and fluid. Each muscle movement activates some sort of
energy in your body, so if you do not move, your energy levels
stagnate and even deplete—both mentally and physically.

Unlike Western thinkers, Eastern societies do not focus solely on the brain when diagnosing and dealing with conditions such as anxiety and depression. Eastern medicines prefer a whole-body perspective. Practitioners see the human body and all its parts as deeply interconnected, so physical aspects are just as important as the mental aspects. In Eastern medicine, the idea of chi, or life energy, is critical to understanding illness. This life energy moves through us at all times. It ebbs and flows naturally as well as in reaction to external circumstances.

How to do it. You can start yoga right now by doing some basic movements. Here are a few to try: Stand and reach up into the air and gently roll your body down to touch your toes. Lie down and stretch your whole body from fingers to toes. Do gentle body twists and roll-ups (like sit-ups) and relax your arms and legs to improve movement and circulation. You'll find many simple demonstrations of yoga asanas or poses in books and on the Internet.

I recommend signing up for a free introductory yoga class at a local studio or community center. Speak to the instructor to learn more about how yoga works and the different kinds of yoga practices. You can then decide if you prefer to do body movement alone at home (perhaps with the help of a video) or to join a regular group.

One example of the power of a body movement is a simple smile. The Vietnamese Zen Buddhist monk Thích Nhất Hạnh recommends practicing "smile yoga," a slight but authentic smile, many times during each day. As he says, "A tiny bud of a smile on your lips nourishes awareness and calms you miraculously." A smile can send a physiological message to your mind that you are safe and free from harm.

What to notice. If you gently reach your arms up or roll your shoulders back, you will feel your lungs expand and energy move down into your entire body. You may notice that you release energy trapped in your head and neck. If you slowly roll down and touch your toes, you will notice tingling all the way down your neck and spine. As you let your body hang down, you can stimulate your legs and feet. Every small movement has the possibility to open up closed joints or tight muscles. After any body movement, you will feel more flexible, fluid and calm, since you are freeing your body to move in the way in which it was designed.

Chapter 2

Your Mind

Adopt a beginner's mind

The Buddha cautioned: The future is always other than you imag-
ined it. He repeatedly stated that you must not start living as
though this moment's main worth lies only in some future benefit.
—Phillip Moffitt, *Dancing with Life*

What it is. There is an old Hindu teaching called the Snake and the
Rope. As the story goes, a man enters a dark room and sees something coiled on the floor. He begins to panic, thinking it is a snake,
but when he turns on the light, he realizes it is just a rope. This tale
teaches us that all too often, due to our habitual thinking, we think
ropes are snakes and thus respond inappropriately. We misinter-
pret situations or circumstances because of outdated, fearful
thoughts, thus causing us even more stress and anxiety.

A powerful mindfulness practice designed to combat this tendancy
is called "Zen mind," or "beginner's mind." In a practical sense, it means
seeing something for the very first time, as if you were a child or a complete beginner. This involves looking at a situation or at a person without
any preconceived notions or judgments. This type of mind is empty and
not clogged with erroneous beliefs or assumptions. It is said to be like
an empty bowl or cup, ready to be filled. Although this mindfulness practice sounds easy, it is difficult. From childhood, we have been filled with
so much information that it's almost impossible to sort out what is real.
So trying on a beginner's mind can be insightful.

How to do it. Go outside during the daytime and look at the sky. Pretend you are a child and you are seeing the sky for the first time. Open your eyes wide, smile, and try to evoke a sense of excitement and curiosity. Simply observe the sky. Try not to label colors as white or blue or the shapes as clouds. Definitely do not try to predict the weather! What do you notice? Do you have any feelings about what you see? Ever wonder how the sky feels or smells? Do the clouds feel heavy or light? Do you want to touch them? Do you recall similar childhood thoughts?

Another way to practice beginner's mind is during a conversation with a friend. Next time you are in a conversation, try to empty your mind of any previous thoughts. Just listen as if you were hearing these words for the very first time. Get excited. Pretend you know nothing about the person or the circumstances. Do not try not to anticipate where the conversation is going. Notice any body language and tone of voice. Do not offer suggestions or leap to conclusions. This not only allows you to see things more vividly and accurately, but allows the other person space so they feel deeply heard.

What to notice. Although adopting a beginner's mind can be fun, you may find it difficult to maintain over time. This is because our minds are continually moving forward or backwards, rarely staying right here, right now. Yet when you adopt a naive, childlike mind-set and attitude, your mind is completely free, open to any possibility. You see things in ways you might never have seen before and you tap pure creativity, since your mind is not blocked by preconceived ideas. It's empowering to realize you no longer have to be a victim of your narrow mind and can choose to look at things in a new and fresh way.

Notice your monkey mind

You don't have to control your thoughts, you just have to stop
letting them control you.
—Dan Millman

What it is. Right now, thousands of thoughts and ideas are cruising through your mind. Most of them are useful, but almost as many are driving you crazy. Much of our mental energy is spent worrying, anticipating and regretting, ruminating and even catastrophizing. So many of our thoughts are on autopilot, filling up space that could be better used for rejuvenation or creative thinking. These thoughts also keep us from being in the moment and seeing what is right in front of us. This thinking is called our "monkey mind." It is like a monkey constantly jumping up and down and all around.

To manage these thousands of not-very-useful thoughts, you must first become aware of them. One powerful mindful way to do this is called "Name that thought." You train yourself to notice your thinking, and then when a thought pops into your head, you simply name it and recognize it as a thought. By doing so, you can stop the thought momentarily and then observe it. This reduces a thought's power and enables you to better manage it.

How to do it. Sit in a chair and settle in. Close your eyes and breathe deeply a few times. Now try to empty your mind of all thoughts.

Eventually, a thought will show up. When a thought pops up, become aware of it. For example, your mind might say things like "I need to get groceries," or "I can't believe June never called me back!" As a thought enters your brain, just notice it. This is a powerful tool, since now you have become the observer of your own thoughts.

After a while, try to label each thought by saying to yourself, "That's a thought!" or "Thinking." Do not try to force the thought out. Just notice it. Although this sounds easy, you must practice this technique often to be able to maintain it on a regular basis. Eventually, however, you will be able to let your thoughts move through your brain without getting stuck. Eventually, "It's just a thought" will flow off your tongue.

What to notice. Do you notice how many thoughts you have? Do you see how many of them keep coming back over and over? Do you notice what happens when you name them? Does this naming take away the power of the thought? You may also notice that thoughts tend to fall into three categories: the future, the past and right now. How many of your thoughts are about the future or the past?

You will slowly realize that most of what is going on in your head is just thinking. Nothing more, nothing less. Once you notice this, you have enormous power to choose whether to ignore your thoughts or to let them go. Keep in mind, however, that the goal of this practice is not to remove all thoughts, but rather to notice what is showing up, give it compassion and let it be.

Practice 13

Live in the now

Thoughts, emotions, moods and memories come and they go,
and the basic newness is always here.
—Pema Chödrön, *Start Where You Are*

What it is. Years ago, while running, a friend and I were discussing author Eckhart Tolle's book *The Power of Now* and the importance of living in the moment. I recall my friend (Diane, another lawyer) stopping abruptly on our remote forest trail and saying, "So, Maureen, what am I supposed to do? Stop running and meditate?" The irony was not lost on me. Here we were, running as fast as we could past all this natural beauty, not really knowing how to *be here while running*. We did not appreciate how our bodies were moving or how the air felt. We did not sense our feet pounding or the shadows cast by the tall trees. We were probably thinking about our post-run shower and our to-do lists.

For some reason, we human beings find it hard to stay in the present moment. There is so much to look forward to and so much of our past to dwell upon, yet when we stay in the here and now, we not only see things in a unique and fresh light, but we free ourselves to be calm, at peace and content.

Pema Chödrön, a well-known Buddhist nun, urges us to simply be right here right now with whatever is going on and to use the breath as a reminder that we are simply human beings breathing, in and out. As we become aware of things like our breath, our bodies, sounds, smells and feelings, we can be more present and alive by noticing them, without allowing them to capture our attention enough to draw us away from this moment.

Living in the "now" has been described as a calm lake. When the weather is windy and the water is wavy and rough, you cannot see into the water. It is murky and dark. When the lake is calm, the surface is smooth and reflects the light, the sky and the clouds. You are able to see deep within the lake because the water is transparent. This is how it feels to be totally in the present. You feel calm, centered and clear-minded, as well as joyful and light.

How to do it. Recall your last bath or shower. Do you remember what you were thinking about during it? More likely than not, you were probably on automatic pilot, allowing your mind to fully engage in things that were nowhere near the shower. Now, for your next bath or shower, do this: Take off your clothes slowly, and step into the shower slowly. Notice the cool air on your skin. Turn the water on and feel your hands around the tap. Watch the water pour down. Step into the water and feel it dripping down your body. When you pick up the soap, feel it and smell it. Empty your mind of all thoughts. Just be here for this very precious time. This is how it feels to live in the now.

Another practice, taught by Thích Nhất Hạnh, is to write the following words on a large piece of paper and post it on your wall: "What am I doing right now?" Each time you read it, you will be forced to pay attention to exactly what you are doing at this precise moment. Are you breathing? Are you thinking about what might happen in a week from now? Are you recalling an event that happened months ago? Are you aware of your surroundings? Are you totally present?

What to notice. It's really quite surprising that we live so much of our lives without being aware of so much that is happening to us and around us. And it can be a radical shift when we choose to focus only on what is happening right now and nothing else. You realize just how much is available to you if you shift your attention to the present moment. You begin to see things much more vividly, as if colors and smells had been introduced into a black and white photograph. Your senses come alive, and you feel truly alive.

Practice 14

Meditate

Meditation is intended to purify the mind. It cleanses the thought process of what can be called psychic irritation, things like greed, hatred, jealousy, which keeps you snarled up in emotional bondage.
—Bhante Gunaratana, *Mindfulness in Plain English*

What it is. In the past, meditation or contemplation was reserved for a few exclusive religious sages. These people used it primarily as a way to get in touch with a higher power. Today, however, almost anyone can meditate almost anywhere, with anyone. And the uses of medication are varied, from simply inducing a state of calm to accessing the subconscious mind.

Although the process of meditation is the cornerstone of Buddhist-style mindfulness, it is not limited to any philosophy, religion or belief system. Many religions, however, believe that through meditation we become awake, conscious or connected with the universe, the ultimate source or God.

Meditation today is used for two main purposes: to create a mental state of calm and to access deeper wisdom. However, the benefits of meditation are wide-ranging. In meditation you sit in silence, learn how to let go, and free yourself from the captivity of your limited mind. Sitting in silence clears out the clutter of compulsive thinking and emotionally charged feelings, thus directly reducing stress and anxiety. At a deeper level, meditation allows us to see ourselves and our struggles more clearly and helps us learn to deal with difficulties with equanimity, rather than impulsiveness.

Although there are many ways to meditate, all involve sitting still and emptying the mind. Each method involves either removing all thoughts completely and entering a meditative state (often by focusing on a mantra or other item) or simply inviting the mind to calm itself by moving from the chaos of thoughts and emotions to quietness and silence. No matter what the practice, the essence is the same. All techniques are designed to provoke calm and center us in the present moment.

How to do it. Sit on the ground or on a chair. You can sit cross-legged on a pillow or on a chair with your feet flat on the floor. Set your posture so you feel grounded but upright—as if you were a majestic mountain or sitting on a throne, with composure and dignity. Lift up your chin and straighten your back so your head is balanced comfortably on top of your neck. Adjust your body until you feel stable. Here are the seven basic points on posture, although the key is to select a posture in which you can be both alert and relaxed.

- Back straight like an arrow
- Legs crossed, or seated in a chair with feet on the ground
- Shoulders relaxed but held up and back
- Chin tucked in slightly
- Eyes closed or gazing a few feet ahead
- Tongue relaxed or gently touching the roof of your mouth
- Lips slightly apart, teeth not clenched

It is important to sit in a way that is dignified and awe-inspiring, not to be slumped or too stiff. In this posture, simply breathe in and out in a relaxed manner. When a thought or feeling arises, allow it to float across your mind. Come back to the breath, over and over, for from 10 to 30 minutes. Because meditation is a lifelong skill, it is useful to read books on the various practices and select the techniques that work best for you.

What to notice. At first this type of sitting in silence in a posture can be awkward and uncomfortable, but your body will adjust over time. You will begin to notice that it is easier to settle in and you will look forward to it. As you sit in silence, you may also become acutely aware of those body parts that feel stiff or tight. If so, gently breathe into those places and release them. Breathe deeply into your belly.

You may also often be taken over by your own crazy mind. On certain days you will find that meditating comes easy, while on others you will find it nearly impossible to calm your body or your mind. On those days, do not force it. Simply come back to a sense of expanding, so feelings and thoughts will be less likely to wreak havoc and can be freed to float by. Meditation is not meant to be torture!

The discipline of meditation is often described as sitting like a mountain. As all sorts of weather—like storms, wind and rain—passes overhead, you remain steady and calm. You are no longer reacting to the external impacts but are simply aware of the continually passing weather and letting it go. You remain calm and steady.

Practice 15

Feel gratitude

Mental habits of judgment and self-criticism can create a virtual prison wherein your work—no matter how successful—never seems good enough.
—Jeffrey Brantley and Wendy Millstine, *Five Good Minutes*

What it is. In our society today we continually feel as if we do not have enough. We think we need more money, more success, more fame and more status. We are on the treadmill of continuous self-improvement and accumulation of education, credentials, experiences and money. We have come to believe that we need "things" to be happy and that we can never have enough. We also believe we are not quite good enough *as we are*. We need to continually excel, go faster and be better to feel good about ourselves. This behavior is driven by one deep mental habit called "scarcity thinking," and it is truly holding us back.

The practice of gratitude is an antidote to this mental compulsion. It is a sense of thankfulness and the feeling that we are sufficient and that we have enough. By feeling gratitude, we are reminded that we already have all we need at this moment and we do not need to constantly improve and continually accumulate things. We slow the desire to propel ourselves forward. After all, we are human beings, not human doings.

Research shows that people who practice gratitude not only increase their sense of happiness but also improve their sense of well-being, peace and calm. This is because, as Buddhists have known for centuries, one of the main causes of human suffering is craving, or wanting for more. When we show gratitude, we stop wanting and feel satisfied with who we are and what we have. We find peace.

How to do it. Experiencing gratitude can be as simple as saying a prayer of grace before dinner or recalling all the things in your life for which you are grateful. One fun practice involves finding a glass jar and placing a label on it: My Gratitude Jar. Cut up small bits of paper (colored is nice!) and stack them beside the jar. Take a few pieces, write something on each that you are grateful for, and place the papers in the jar. Add to this jar daily until it is full. Each week, empty it out and read each note aloud, then start again. Another version of this practice involves writing in a "gratitude journal" where you list and reflect on all the things you are grateful for.

What to notice. You will likely walk away from this practice with an enhanced sense of contentment. You may even feel more generous and feel like donating your time or your old clothes to a charity. If you are the average person living in North America, you likely have enough. You probably have food, shelter and your health. If you have more than these basics, then feeling gratitude will make you feel enormously blessed. As I often say, "It was just the luck of the draw that I was born here and not in Calcutta, India."

Practice 16

Practice affirmations

We can free ourselves from negative influences, harmful habits and the effects of long term conditioning by reprogramming our subconscious mind with positive suggestions, known as affirmations.
—Paul Roland, *How to Meditate*

What it is. Affirmations are simply positive suggestions. Whether written or spoken, they are designed to program our minds with constructive thoughts and break harmful mental habits. In simple terms, they replace fearful or destructive thoughts with positive or constructive thoughts.

Although many books have been written on the power of affirmations, in essence they are a simple tool to convince your mind that you are truly powerful and can make things happen. Affirmations were promoted in the 1970s by cognitive-behavioral psychologists who used them in replacing their clients' negative thinking patterns with positive ones. The theory is that if we change our thoughts, our behavior will change as well.

More recent research, however, shows that affirmations are even more impactful. When worded in a particular way, they become more than just positive thinking and can lead to a shift in reality—in our brains and in our experiences. Many people have found that affirmations said repeatedly with emotion can manifest surprising things or create a different reality in their lives.

How to do it. Cut a piece of letter-size paper into six smaller pieces, like business cards. On each card, write your own personal affirmation. Here are a few examples:

- "I am on my true path and every day I am becoming more skilled."
- "I am perfectly acceptable as I am."
- "There is plenty for everybody."
- "I am calm and centered."
- "I am perfect just as I am."

The phrases should be short and worded in the present tense—as if you have already achieved them. For each one, try to conjure up an image in your mind and bring it to your attention several times a day over several weeks. If you have difficulty writing down affirmations, this may indicate a block in your attitude. In this case you might want to "Fake it until you make it" and see what happens.

Louise Hay (Hay House Publishing) sells beautiful boxed sets of affirmation cards that can be read at any time. One of the best-known affirmations is the phrase "Every day, in every way, I am becoming better and better," but the most effective affirmations are the phrases you create in your own words.

What to notice. When you first write out or read an affirmation, you may feel silly. For many people, the practice feels like naive wishful thinking or even a waste of time. This is because we were told as young children to not get our hopes up and that it's wasteful and frivolous to dream. If you feel this way, try to move past it. Write the affirmations in private. The truth is that your brain will believe almost exactly what you tell it to, so it's a shame to not benefit from this powerful tool. After all, there is no harm in trying. An affirmation is only a mental shift and takes only a few minutes.

Visualize

Imagination is more important than knowledge.
—Albert Einstein

What it is. Years ago I was introduced to the following exercise. Stand still and hold out an empty hand in front of you, palm up. Now imagine that you have a juicy lemon slice in your hand and it is dripping onto your fingers. It looks like the type of wedges you might find in a restaurant or bar. Now move your hand closer to your mouth, focusing completely on the lemon. As you move your hand closer to your mouth, do you start to salivate? If so, you have experienced visualization.

Visualizing is imagining, or seeing through the mind's eye. It is simply creating something that does not yet exist in reality. Similar to daydreaming, we all have this ability yet most people don't know how to use it or how powerful it can be. For example, when we're stressed out we tend to shut down our imagination and get tunnel vision. We feel trapped and think there is no way out. We can't possibly imagine another scenario, yet this is the very thing that can help. You can visualize a beautiful flower garden or a waterfall, and your body will notably relax. You can visualize your own success or overcoming an obstacle, and your confidence will increase.

Planting a vision in your mind not only causes your body to think the vision is real, but can even produce feelings and behaviors consistent with that vision. In effect, you are programming your mind by creating images. This is why so many people, especially athletes, use visualization on a regular basis. Many of the world's religious traditions use visualization as a way to bring about transformation in consciousness. Recently, some have suggested that the very act of visualizing can manifest things into reality. Called the "law of attraction," this is the subject of many books. The Swiss psychologist Carl Jung also used visualization to access the unconscious mind and heal negative mental conditioning.

How to do it. Find a quiet place to sit. Close your eyes and breathe deeply. Recall a place you have been that brought you great joy or relaxation, such as a lakeside, a meadow or a park. Imagine exactly where you are sitting. How does it feel? Picture the place in your mind and notice your surroundings. Listen for the sounds. Feel the air against your skin. Now breathe it all in. Feel it through your entire body. Notice how your body responds.

Another practice is to close your eyes for a minute. Imagine you are carrying a heavy backpack full of rocks. You approach a lush meadow beside a calm pool of water. It is a windless day. You drop your pack onto the ground. You stand up straight and roll your shoulders backwards. You feel the release of tension. Breathe deeply and let out your breath slowly. Your pack represents your past. You are free to go on with your day feeling calm and lighter.

What to notice. When you visualize something positive, neuro-transmitters are activated in your brain, which makes you *feel* good. This helps at a physiological level to relax muscles, at a psychological level to shift thinking, and at an emotional level to release energy attached to feelings. Dreaming while awake is like taking an instant happy pill. For example, if you visualize yourself as an open-hearted and compassionate person, you are better able to let go of selfishness or weakness. If you visualize being loved, accepted and acknowledged, you will have a better sense of self-acceptance.

Practice 18

Avoid assumptions

*People are fundamentally good, though no one has bothered to
tell most of them.*
—Gandhi

What it is. We humans are quick to make grand, sweeping assumptions—about pretty much everything. We assume that dark clouds mean rain and that a headache indicates a tumor. Although we are all skilled at observing, we often shut down this ability in favor of judging situations and leaping to conclusions with our busy and often biased mind. And this all happens in an instant, without us even being aware of it.

We cause ourselves enormous strain by assuming we know what others are thinking, particularly about us. If we see an eye-roll, for example, we automatically assume someone thinks we are stupid or that person is making fun of us. If we see two people gossiping in a corner, we assume they are gossiping about us. This is what I call "going into other people's brains," and it can get you into enormous trouble and stress, all unnecessarily. Marshall Rosenberg, the late American psychologist and author of *Nonviolent Communication*, said we could all save ourselves a huge amount of anxiety if we simply stopped trying to imagine what others are thinking. It is not only not possible to know what they are thinking, but can also be very harmful to ourselves.

Assuming is just a mental habit and therefore it can be changed. The more we notice our assumptions and faulty thinking, the better we are able to prevent misunderstandings and avoid any harm that flows from these thoughts. We can challenge our assumptions.

How to do it. Try to remember your first day at a new school as a child. Do you remember seeing all the new and different faces of strangers? Do you recall your teacher? Do remember what the children were wearing? Do you remember your very first impressions? Try to recall some of the specific things that passed through your mind, like "He's fat, I bet he eats a lot," or "She's wearing an old dress and muddy boots. I bet her parents are poor," or "He has expensive clothes. I bet he is a snob!" Now try to imagine if you made no assumptions about these children at all. Notice how that feels. After that, shift again and imagine what would happen if you assumed only good things about each person.

What to notice. Initially, you may be shocked at the number of assumptions you make—all unconsciously. However, don't be too hard on yourself, because most assumptions arise from old, unchallenged thought patterns working overtime. Try to develop the skill of noticing your preconceived ideas and gently reining them in. The goal is not to remove all of your assumptions, but rather to become conscious enough to be able to choose which ones are helpful and which ones are not.

Practice 19

Find your passion

If one advances confidently in the direction of his dreams, and endeavors to live the life which he has imagined, he will be met with success in uncommon hours.
—Ralph Waldo Emerson

What it is. A few years ago, after practicing law for many years, I decided to quit and find a job that was better matched to my skills and interests. I read more than two hundred books on careers, life purpose, psychology and spirituality. I came to realize that one of the most important steps in finding happiness in life was to uncover my passion, or what I cared most about. Indeed, research shows that people with a sense of purpose or meaning are happier and more resilient in the face of stress. It can be soothing and calming to know that you have a purpose bigger than yourself and that your life is important. I ended up writing a book on the topic and was able to share what I had learned. The book is *titled If Not Now When? Create a Life and Career with Purpose and Passion.*

Many people live their entire lives and never consider their life purpose. Driven by the need to survive and earn money, they rarely reflect on whether their work is good for them or is contributing to society in a positive way. In fact, many people think work is, by definition, stressful and would say it's silly to try to find work that you love. Although some consider finding their passion a waste of time, when difficulties arise, and they always do, having goals and a sense of direction can act as a life preserver. Your passion keeps you afloat in rough waters and acts as a beacon or compass when you are feeling lost.

How to do it. In my book *What's Next?*, I recommend five steps to help you discover your life purpose. The two most relevant here are to create a "vision" by imagining your ideal life and to define your personal "mission statement." Here is a summary of these steps.

To create your vision, imagine yourself twenty years from now. Imagine what you are doing and who you are with. Imagine how you feel and how others are responding to you. Include all the things you always hoped to have, like friends, family and a safe home. Write down a detailed description or create a poster from images and words. This is your vision. Reflect on it often and let it sink in.

Next, create your mission statement by reflecting on the things you care mostly deeply about. Is it poverty? Homelessness? Justice? Animals? Art? What would you talk about on national TV if given five minutes of airtime? Now try to fill in the blanks in the following statements: I would be most happy if I could help _____ (who) to _____ (topic or problem). For example, I would be most happy if I could help <u>pet owners</u> to <u>keep their dogs fit and healthy without spending much</u>. This is your very rough mission statement, which you can refine over time. When you put the results of these two steps together, you will have a sense of where you want to end up (vision) and what you want to do to get there (mission).

What to notice. You may notice that many of these ideas were already in your head, but had never been fully articulated in a concise and practical way. By putting into words your purpose, you may feel grounded and motivated. You may also feel powerful, in control, and with a sense of hope for the future, all of which reduces the discomfort or stress of not knowing what the future will bring.

Practice 20

Stop for a sacred pause

How simple it is to see that all the worry in the world cannot control the future. How simple it is to see that we can only be happy now. And that there will never be a time when it is not now.

—Gerald Jampolsky, *Love is Letting go of Fear*

What it is. Sometimes the quickest way to reduce stress is to simply stop. Stop thinking. Stop eating your dinner. Stop reading. Meditation expert Tara Brach introduced the idea of the "sacred pause" as a first step to "radical acceptance" (the title of her book). The sacred pause is a suspension of activity, a temporary disengagement when we are no longer moving toward a goal. It can happen at any time in the day. You simply stop. Some people use pop-up software or an alarm to remind them each hour to simply stop and observe what is happening. In their *Mindfulness-Based Stress Reduction Workbook*, Bob Stahl and Elisha Goldstein use the acronym STOP, which stands for Stop, Take a breath, Observe and Proceed.

How to do it. At random times during the day, stop for a minute and consider whether you are being mindful. Are you breathing fully? Are your shoulders relaxed? Are you tense and anxious? You may wish to use your hands as anchors or reminders to be present.

Touch your palms and press them together, saying, "Thank you, hands." Press your hands down on your chair and say, "Oh, my goodness, I almost forgot I was here. I almost forgot how precious this moment is." Take a few deep breaths and go back to what you were doing.

What to notice. When you stop and breathe, you physically slow down and relax your body. As you breathe in and out, you are effectively releasing worry and tension. When you resume activities, you will do so with increased presence and will be more clear-minded when thinking and when making decisions.

Chapter 3

Your Heart

Practice 21

Notice your feelings

Freedom begins when we pause and pay attention to our experience.
—Tara Brach, *Radical Acceptance*

What it is. In our society we reject most emotions. We only allow crying when we experience a life crisis, like a death or divorce. Because of this, when we feel sad or broken-hearted or feel like crying, we tend to push the feelings away. We think our feelings are inappropriate or out of proportion and tell ourselves we should show more self-control. Yet feeling our emotions is a critical part of our psychological and physical well-being. Unfortunately, many of us struggle between being emotionally closed, in complete fear of feelings and being emotionally overwhelmed by them.

Eve Ensler, activist and playwright, gave a popular YouTube talk, "I Am an Emotional Creature." This talk vividly demonstrates the power of emotions and what they look like in their most profound form. It encourages us to accept and value all of our emotional capacities.

In mindfulness, allowing emotions to surface is considered natural and normal. We are encouraged to feel them and accept them even if we choose not to act upon them. The emotions are not only necessary to human development, but are also informative and powerful openings. Just below the surface of a feeling we often discover our deepest human longings and needs, such as our longing to be loved and to belong, as well as our need to contribute and feel needed. When we allow ourselves to tap into this longing and accept it, we open a doorway to accepting ourselves. We are then better able to find peace and love.

The secret to handling emotions is to not overreact with a knee-jerk response or under-react by collapsing, but to simply notice them, accept them and listen to them.

How to do it. Marshall Rosenberg, an internationally renowned conflict resolution expert, taught us how to feel and define our emotions through an increased vocabulary. He believed that once we can articulate how we are feeling, we are better able to get to the real source of our own needs and where those needs conflict with others. In his books he included full pages of words that describe emotions (like frustrated, irritated, shamed, flustered, etc.). It's helpful to see just how many emotions there are and how each one feels different. Rather than simply thinking we are angry (a very generic and common emotion), we can instead say we are annoyed, depressed or overwhelmed. Next time you get in an argument, try to articulate your feelings and write them down. See if you can better understand the reasons for the argument.

What to notice. It's fantastic when you have a good vocabulary of emotions. Not only can you better read others' emotions, but you are better able to diagnose your own feelings and explain them to others. We have on our fridge a full page of different facial expressions. It was given to us when our children were young so they could learn how to talk about emotions and recognize emotions in others. The page of expressions is a wonderful tool for teaching empathy, and it's a useful skill to notice that one small lift of an eye can make a person look angry rather than curious.

Practice 22

Pay attention to stress

The advantage of emotions is that they lead us astray.
—Oscar Wilde

What it is. All humans feel emotional pain as well as physical pain. When we feel physical pain, we call a doctor or mend it on our own. When we feel emotional pain, we often tend to deny it or avoid it. We tell ourselves that things are not really that bad. We watch TV, we drink, and we work—anything to not feel the hurt. Yet we know intuitively that this pain might be telling us something. So rather than ignore it, a more mindful approach is to simply notice it without running from it. Often by simply noticing it and naming the feeling (e.g., "There is my anxiety again"), you are able to release it, allowing your body to relax so you can remain calm until the peak passes.

If we can do this, we are one step closer to accepting our emotional pain and perhaps listening to what it has to say. For example, emotional pain can emerge from a simple thought, like dread, or from a basic feeling, like frustration. By being mindful, we not only feel our pain, but also understand its relationship to our thoughts and other feelings. When we attend closely to our emotional pain, we begin to understand ourselves and how we cause pain and are impacted by pain. As a result, we become more skilled at managing these intense feelings and preventing them from causing harm.

How to do it. Settle into your body completely. Take a deep breath. Think back on a time when you were emotionally overwhelmed or frustrated. Perhaps you got upset or "lost it" when someone said or did something. Now go back and rewind the mental tape. Try to re-call three things. First try to recall your *bodily sensations* (e.g., you heart rate). Then try to recall your *feelings* (e.g., frustration). Then try to recall your *thoughts* (e.g., "He does not care about me"). Notice how each of these is distinct. Notice as well how one leads directly to the other.

As you do this practice, try to find words to describe how you felt in the moment, such as "I felt my heart rate rising," "I felt agitated, fearful and anxious," or "I felt the urge to run and hide." These words help you to unpack complex combinations of thoughts and feelings and thus make them more manageable. You can also try this prac-tice when you are happy, saying something like "I sense my body relaxing," or "I feel safe and at ease."

What to notice. You may be surprised by what you learn about yourself through your emotional intelligence. You may notice how certain things trigger you, over and over. Patterns may emerge. You may notice the escalation of emotions from a slight tension to full-out yelling. You might notice missed opportunities to de-escalate the situation. And although it might seem opposite to what you have done in the past, the mindful way to deal with heightened emotions is to show them compassion. It does not help to berate yourself for having them. In Zen Buddhism there is a saying, "Pain is inevitable, but suffering is optional."

Practice 23

Attend to your pain

*The trouble with ordinary reality is that a lot of it is dull so we
long ago decided to leave it for somewhere better.*
—Charles Tart, *Living the Mindful Life*

What it is. In 1979, Jon Kabat-Zinn, a molecular biologist, founded the MBSR (Mindfulness-Based Stress Reduction) program at the University of Massachusetts Medical Center. His research on anxiety and chronic pain showed significant reductions in stress for those who practiced mindfulness and meditation. That eight-week program is now to be found in over 250 hospitals in the United States.

A fundamental principal in the MBSR program is learning to sit with the pain and not run from it. This involves becoming aware of the pain without allowing it to take over—learning how to label it, how to watch it while letting all the thoughts we have about it come and go. Although MBSR teaches you how to relax into the pain, the pain does not necessarily go away. However, much of the suffering does. This is accomplished by asking your body, "What needs attention (or love) right now?" When we acknowledge and attend to our pain without trying to push it away, we can begin to wake up and hear what our body really needs.

How to do it. You can do this practice with either physical pain or emotional pain. For physical pain, try to recall a recent minor trauma, like a headache or a cut on your finger. Recall how it felt and how you reacted to the pain. Did you freak out or dramatize it? Did you calmly locate a bandage? For emotional pain, try to recall a recent feeling—perhaps of being embarrassed. Maybe you did something silly or wrong and someone made fun of you. Try to recall exactly how it felt in your body. Was it a pit in your stomach or tightness in your throat? Did you try to avoid the feeling? What did you think about? Did you dwell on your emotional triggers and create more angst? Did you rationalize it away?

Now try the ABC approach. Accept it, breathe into it, and show self-compassion. With both types of pain, imagine sitting calmly and simply acknowledging that it is happening. Then take a few deep breaths (assuming that blood is not gushing out of your wound) and then imagine wrapping your arms around yourself in a compassionate hug. Now try to imagine labeling your pain as "a small cut" or "a sense of being ashamed." Imagine that you can observe your pain or hurt without being completely carried away by your feelings.

What to notice. By accepting your pain, breathing into it, and show-ing self-compassion, you will begin to experience your pain differently. At the minimum, you will be able to slow down your au-tomatic, knee-jerk reaction and in doing so create a space to allow for new responses to your pain. As you become more self-aware, you may be able to distinguish between the feeling associated with the direct "pain" and the feeling associated with your struggle to end the pain or "suffering." If nothing else, you may begin to feel a sense of control over your direct body-based sensations and gut reactions. They no longer control you.

Practice 24

Listen to your sadness

Despite the out-of-control feelings you may experience when you cry, doing so frees your mind and body from the constant need to be in control of your feelings.
—Jeffrey Brantley and Wendy Millstine, *Five Good Minutes*

What it is. Sadness and loneliness are two of the most basic human experiences—deeply felt emotions that are often our most powerful teachers. Yet in our society not many people want to talk about these feelings. Unlike other emotions, like anger or frustration, which are felt more on the surface and tend to be directed outward, these deep emotions are often directed inward—and may be at the root of our other emotions.

For example, after completely "melting down" or "losing it," you may find yourself alone and wondering what happened. At that time you may feel deeply sad and all alone. You may be angry at yourself for behaving badly and frustrated at not seeing it unfold. But lurking beneath these surface emotions is a deeper sense of disconnection.

In essence, our deep sadness comes from the harm we have caused to our relationships and to ourselves. Mindfulness urges you to listen closely to this sadness since it often provides the wisdom to understand not only why you got so angry, but more importantly, how you can finally heal from this anger and become fully human, which involves reconnecting with yourself and others. Indeed, Parker Palmer, a well-known educational philosopher, once defined depression as disconnection either from yourself or from others.

How to do it. Next time you feel sad, do not ask yourself why you are sad. Do not try to figure out the reasons for your sadness. Just say to yourself, "I have the sensation of sadness." Then try to locate this feeling in your body. Is it in your head? In your chest? In your throat? Try to breathe into this part of your body and ask yourself, "Tell me, sadness: What are you trying to tell me right now? What is it that I need to know to allow me to grow?" Your sadness may reply with something like "Stop being so hard on yourself. Arguments happen," or "You are lovable and perfect just as you are." Wait for an answer, and if you fall asleep, the answer may come in your dreams or upon waking.

What to notice. We all feel sad sometimes and this is okay. If you do not push away your sadness, you will notice that your struggle and tension decrease. When you accept being sad, you gain immediate relief, and by sitting with the sadness, you can gain relief for even longer. Sadness often masks unconscious feelings that may need more attention and healing. If so, the sadness can be seen as a gift, an opportunity to finally heal old wounds that keep causing you anxiety, and then move on.

Practice 25

Befriend yourself

It appears to be part of the human condition that many of us are occasionally plagued with a lack of self-love and compassion. How many times have you told yourself things like 'I should have done better?' The fact is, nearly everyone is plagued by a nasty, small-minded, fearful critic that judges them day in and day out.
—Donald Altman, *The Mindfulness Code*

What it is. Many of us are so cruel to ourselves. We speak to ourselves in a way we would never speak to a friend—or even an enemy! We judge ourselves constantly and often. We tell ourselves we are stupid, bad and inconsiderate. We blame ourselves for anything that goes wrong. We blame ourselves for being bad parents, bad spouses and bad friends. This voice can be unrelenting. This is called the self-judge and has its roots in our upbringing.

When you were a child, you learned all about what is good and what is bad, what is right and what is wrong, what is appropriate behavior and what is not. Eating healthy foods is good; eating candy is bad. Getting along with your sister is good; gossip is bad.

But something harmful happened in the midst of all this learning. Many of us came to think that if we did something "bad" we were "bad" people. In fact, our parents and teachers, not knowing better, often said things like "good girl" or "bad boy" (often accompanied by punishment), reinforcing this feeling of not being a good child. Over time, these self-assessments sunk in and many of us still can't shake the feeling of not being "good enough," of being unlovable or of feeling undeserving. And this thinking can cause trouble in our lives, for when we reject ourselves, we not only harm ourselves, but also harm those around us.

The good news is that this self-hate is just a mental habit and your self-judge can be managed. The mindful way to do this is by noticing the judge and not allowing it to take over.

How to do it. One common word used by the self-judge is "should." When you hear yourself say something like "I shouldn't have got-ten so angry," or "I shouldn't have spoken so much," just notice it. When you say "should," you are actually rejecting parts of yourself and reinforcing your sense of unworthiness. It's like saying, "There is something wrong with me." It harms you every time you say it.

A mindful technique is to simply replace every "should" with a "could." When you think you have done something inappropriate or wrong, first acknowledge your behavior without judging and then be kind to yourself. Self-reflect, but in a kind way. For example, you might say, "I feel bad for speaking so much. I know I spoke more than the others, but I choose to not beat myself up this time. I feel proud for having noticed my self-judge. I will show myself compas-sion and could try to listen more at the next meeting."

What to notice. You may be surprised to find how often you judge yourself and find great relief in simply recognizing that your judge is just a thought, and not reality. You may be successful in telling the judge to go away, but if you welcome the judge calmly, you may also notice that it is actually trying to help you, in a weird kind of way. Psychologists call this suffering the "protective ego," who thinks that self-criticism will somehow protect you from harm. When you are mindful, you can reject this voice and take on a more enlightened voice of self-compassion. In this way you accept your-self as an evolving human being. You are learning through self-reflection and constructive (not destructive) feedback.

Practice 26

Go on a media diet

In ad after ad, girls are urged to be "barely there"—beautiful but silent. Many ads in teen magazines feature girls and young women in very passive poses, limp, doll-like, sometimes acting like little girls...
—Jean Kilbourne

What it is. Since I have two teen daughters, we often have family discussions about the impact of media on our behavior, and particularly on our shopping habits. I am sure we women could save thousands of dollars if we were not subjected to continual messages about beauty.

The media affects us in ways we do not fully comprehend. Advertising tells us that we are not pretty enough or slim enough. Television sitcoms tell us our dysfunctional relationships are normal. Radio tells us violence and aggression are fun and sexy. All of this information is fed to us every day in big and small doses, and we barely even notice it. The media tells us what to eat, what to drive and how to behave. It places massive pressures and expectations on each of us, which causes us all stress and anxiety.

We are also addicted to the media. We crave the news and feel out of touch when we don't know what is going on in our world. The problem is that most of the news is not entirely relevant and can be harmful to us. Reports on the violence, the wars, the poverty and abuse of power never end. Without realizing it, through too much exposure to media, we become overly fearful and stressed out. Monitoring our media use and going on a media diet can help.

How to do it. Here are two ways to recognize the ways that media impacts you. First, just notice what you are thinking and feeling when you read or watch the news. Do you feel an urge to buy something after reading an advertisement? Do you decide to dress differently after watching a television show? Another exercise is to not use the Internet or read any newspapers or magazines for one full day. Do not watch television or listen to the radio. Do not check your Twitter or Facebook accounts. Notice how differently you feel and notice the things you do when media is not available.

What to notice. You may begin to notice your body sensations when watching or reading media. Your heart rate might go up. When you stop reading the violent news, you might notice relief at not having to see the murders and tragedies. You may notice that you are calmer and less agitated. You may also notice that the amount of useful information you consume is a very small percentage of all that you take in. You may learn to be more selective and not so passive when reading and watching media—a more conscious and critical consumer.

Practice 27

Practice loving-kindness

Knowing that our words can either heal or hurt, we can strive to use words mindfully and wisely—thus elevating daily language from the mundane to the spiritual.
—Donald Altman, *The Mindfulness Code*

What it is. As humans, we have come to think of hatred as normal. We hate ourselves when we make mistakes and we hate others when they hurt us. Yet the cost of hatred is huge. The amount of energy exerted to carry it around is high, and all that nasty berating of ourselves and others takes a significant toll on our self-esteem and destroys relationships. Hatred is just not healthy.

The practice of loving-kindness is an antidote to this hatred. When we are mindful, we notice hatred in its many forms, recognize its harmful effects, and commit to showing loving-kindness as much as possible.

Loving-kindness, called *mettā* in Sanskrit, is one of the most popular meditation techniques. It is unconditional well-wishing and open-hearted nurturing of ourselves and others, just as we are. When we practice loving-kindness, we learn to treat ourselves and others better, putting aside criticism and hatred and replacing them with love and compassion. This practice is extraordinarily easy yet extraordinarily powerful. It is designed to open your heart to love, compassion and empathy.

How to do it. The most basic loving-kindness meditation involves repeating the following four phrases whenever you can:

> May I be safe.
> May I be healthy.
> May I have freedom from worries.
> May I be at peace.

This is the self-directed version, whereas the more robust version involves saying these or similar phrases toward others. First you insert the name of those close to you (e.g., "May Jim be safe. May Jim be healthy," etc.) and then the names of those you dislike. Eventually, you repeat these phrases to the whole world. You can revise the phrases so they feel right to you and are easy to recite. For example, you might say, "May I be loved. May I be calm," and so on. Another quick version of this practice is to simply smile gently at someone who seems unhappy or irritated. This motion frees you (and them) from getting stuck in judging.

What to notice. If you say the above phases with deep compassion, you will feel your whole body melt. You may realize that you have needed to hear these words because in our crazy world, we rarely hear them. If you direct the words to those you do not like, you will feel your anger or hatred decrease. This is because your words are reflecting a deeper wish from your heart and thus can overpower your mind (which has convinced you that you do not care about others). As a small note, although loving-kindness looks easy, for most of us the task of truly loving ourselves and loving those who are difficult is a lifelong journey.

Practice 28

Notice the judge

*As you come to appreciate and accept that you are imperfectly
perfect, you can extend this attitude to others.*
—Bob Stahl and Elisha Goldstein, *A Mindfulness-Based Stress
Reduction Workbook*

What it is. One of the main reasons why we experience so much conflict in our lives is because we tend to label certain people or groups as
"bad" or "evil." We judge them as having a permanent flaw. We say
things like "He is mean," "She is nasty," "They are evil." When we practice mindfulness, we realize two problems with this labeling. This habit
usually closes us to any possible reconciliation and healing, but worse,
it causes us to carry around a cloud of fear and hatred that actually
causes more harm.

In mindfulness, we come to realize that this type of judging is
harmful to ourselves and in many cases, does not even impact the
person we judge. When we practice mindfulness, we also notice
that our judging of others is often related to our own brutal self-
judging.

In their *Mindfulness-Based Stress Reduction Workbook*, Stahl
and Goldstein mention a story about the Zen master Norman
Fischer. He decided to translate the Book of Psalms from the Bible
into a Buddhist perspective (*Opening to You*, published in 2002). By
simply changing words such as "wicked" to "heedless" and "un-

righteous" to "unmindful," he shifted the entire thrust of the Bible, from judging (of enemies as bad or evil) to accepting (as regular humans who were simply unskilled or unmindful). By shifting your words you too can learn to suspend your judge and begin to see everyone as simply human beings trying to get their needs met.

How to do it. Find a quiet place and sit down. Take a few deep breaths. Now think of a recent fight with someone you know well, like a relative or a close friend. Recall what was said. Recall what you said. Recall how you felt. Do you recall judging the other person as selfish, ignorant, obnoxious, and so on? What if instead of judging this person you said to yourself (about them), "You are an evolving human just like me. I want to understand you and will try my best to be open to your perspective." This might be hard to do, yet it is the very thing you would like another person to say to you when you feel they dislike you! In each situation of conflict, you can choose not to label the other person but instead to think of that person as kind and caring. This can be particularly hard to do when you are feeling attacked, yet it diffuses negative energy, and this type of mirroring acts to empower you. One sentence I often tell myself when I am really mad at someone is: "Perhaps this person has the best intentions, but is behaving this way because their father just died." Having said this, I add that you must always maintain healthy boundaries when dealing with others.

What to notice. Letting go of judging is amazingly powerful. It feels so great to not be controlled by your own anger and fear. You feel you are in control again and realize that you have been investing a huge amount of energy in your anger at other people when you don't need to. To let it go is extremely helpful at relieving stress and slowly you also notice that you can stop judging yourself, too.

Practice 29

Accept the good and the bad

It's important to realize that meditation is not trying to get away
from where you are. Relating to your body is one of the most
valuable lessons to be learned.
—Jane Hope, *The Meditation Year*

What it is. Terrible things happen every day. Your dog might die. Your friend might get mad at you. When bad things happen, our main automatic human impulse is to avoid those bad things and the feelings that accompany them. We either run away as fast as possible, pretend they did not happen or hide. We also engage in "positive thinking" to the point where we simply deny that anything is wrong. We push all negative feelings and thoughts to the bottom of our feet. And the great thing is that this strategy works very well—for about 10 minutes. Then we feel terrible. What we fail to realize is that this aversion to painful events actually causes us more suffering. You know the saying, "What you resist persists." Although denial provides short-term relief, in most cases the bad things linger and resurface. Eventually, we run out of places to hide.

The more mindful way to deal with terrible things is to simply accept them, without rejecting them or wallowing in them. Like a neutral stance, this means listening to what is happening without ignoring it or getting stuck in it. This practice releases our mind's grip, and tension almost immediately dissolves. Indeed, modern psychotherapies now incorporate "acceptance therapy" when help-ing people deal with serious anxiety and trauma. They teach us that pushing back often makes our feelings worse, and gently and compassionately facing them is much more therapeutic.

In Patti Digh's book *Life Is a Verb*, she suggests that we each try to accept things that are difficult for us. Like a friend who talks too much or a teacher who is hard on his students. She suggests simp-ly seeing these as differences to embrace, not problems. One way to stay open to difficulties or differences is by saying out loud: "Help me understand this person or situation," which places you in an open and curious state of mind.

How to do it. For an entire day, try to accept everything that hap-pens, whether good, bad or ugly. Accept yourself to start with. Accept all of your warts, mistakes and awkwardness. Accept those around you, particularly those you might find difficult. Accept de-lays and inconveniences. You don't have to do anything other than just notice how it feels. Here is an affirmation you can repeat to yourself daily that might help: "I accept that both good and bad things happen in my life and both are okay. I accept them all." You might want to read the "Daily Prayer of Acceptance" once a week. You will find it at the end of this book.

What to notice. When you accept yourself completely, it will feel as if you have lifted the weight of the world off your shoulders. Until you feel this completely, you may not have realized just how unac-cepting you were. As children, we are rarely taught unconditional self-love. In fact, the vast majority of our lifelong learning and edu-cation involves focusing on our failings. Given this, it's no wonder we struggle with self-acceptance. When you accept the good and the bad, you become truly free from so many of life's struggles. This does not mean lying down and giving up, but rather, refusing to be controlled by your resentment.

Practice 30

Try compassion

*Think of happiness as a deep ocean. The surface may be chop-
py, but the bottom is always calm. Similarly there are days
when a deeply happy person may feel sad—for example he sees
people suffering—but underneath that sadness, there is a large
depth of unwavering happiness.*
— Matthieu Ricard

What it is. We are all searching for happiness. We spend much of
our time chasing pleasure and avoiding discomfort. There is so
much written about happiness these days—covering topics from
subjective well-being to longevity.

We know there is short-term happiness and long-term happiness. We can gain short-term happiness through things like ice
cream and quick thrills. Yet these are things that tend to come and
go, often leaving us with an empty feeling or even further craving
for the highs. We can gain long-term happiness, which is more sus-
tainable, by doing things that are meaningful and contributing to
something bigger than ourselves. However, it seems that the most
joy experienced by human beings comes in the form of loving relationships, and specifically compassion.

In his book *Search Inside Yourself,* Chade-Meng Tan says, "The
happiest state can only be achieved with compassion, which requires engagement in real life with real people." Therefore, our

mindful practices cannot be limited to sitting alone on a pillow, but also need to involve activating our compassion or engaging with the world.

How to do it. Finding happiness through compassion can be achieved on three levels: with the head (sympathy), with the heart (empathy) and through action (compassion). You can tap your compassion by simply realizing that others are in pain (even if it feels terrible). This simple act of noticing activates your sense of sympathy and triggers a deeply human response, recognizing that we all suffer at some point. The second level involves feeling empathy and involves your emotions or heart. This means actually feeling how others might feel. The third level involves taking action in response to your thoughts and feelings. This means finding concrete ways to show compassion and concern for the well-being and suffering of others. Examples include buying groceries for an older neighbor or volunteering at a food bank.

What to notice. As you begin opening up your heart to others, you will notice several things. The first is that you are not completely smothered or overwhelmed by the suffering of others. Practicing compassion is not as scary as you might think. You may also notice that when you show compassion for others, you mirror compassion toward yourself. Your heart grows bigger for others and for yourself. In other words, you increase your capacity to hold both pain and pleasure.

Chapter 4

Your World

Practice 31

Listen and be heard

Perhaps the most valuable gift we can offer another person is our whole hearted attention.
—Jeffrey Brantley and Wendy Millstine, *Five Good Minutes*

What it is. Those who have visited a counsellor or therapist know the power of being heard. When someone fully listens to us, we not only feel heard, but also acknowledged, accepted and connected. By being truly seen as a vulnerable human being, we experience a sensation almost like love. And this makes us feel truly alive.

Listening and being listened to are essential to feeling loved and accepted as a human being. When we "feel felt," we gain a better sense of connection as well as a deep sense of relatedness and belonging—two critical human needs.

If you watch a mother comforting her child, you will notice that her body is completely soft. Her shoulders are down and her arms are either open or embracing the child. You will notice as well that even her eyes are soft. These "soft eyes" are the ones I used for many years as a lawyer to resolve conflicts and the ones I use when I am dealing with someone who is upset. What these soft eyes tell the other person is not only that you care, but more importantly that you accept them completely. Even if you may not understand them, you believe them and acknowledge their reality. When you use soft eyes, time seems to slow down and your senses seem more alert. Judgment and criticism seem to melt away.

Typically, however, we are so stressed that we have no energy or capacity to listen. When our primitive "fight or flight" response is activated, we tend to shift into "protection mode" and turn inward, rather that outward. Yet, on occasions when we have the skill and capacity to listen and understand, we find that we are better able to center ourselves and respond in a calmer manner.

How to do it. One popular mindful practice is called "active listening," or listening with your whole body. This involves teaming up with another person and simply listening to each other for three minutes each, entirely uninterrupted. Resist the urge to fill in any gaps. Try to feel what the other is feeling and try to reflect that feeling back, without words. When doing so, you can notice how your bodies are more together or apart. You might also notice urges to speak, so practice stopping them before they become an interruption. In a practice session, it's fun to try to sense in your body any tension and use the time to practice breathing calmly. This can be tough to do in real life.

What to notice. When you listen to someone completely, you may notice that you have no thoughts in your head, no ideas about what the person is about to say, and no thoughts about your similar experiences. It's as if you only have room in your brain to hear exactly what they are trying to say. Your mind's full-time job is to make sense of what is being expressed. It has no time to come up with crafted questions and wise responses. You may come to see that, as you let your own ideas and opinions go, you will be better able to focus completely on the other person. You will be better able to truly see and understand the other person. When you yourself feel heard, you feel loved.

Practice 32

Speak mindfully

Words are like living clay with which we shape our relationships.
Wise speech can build trust; unkind speech can cause enduring
damage.
—Donald Altman, *The Mindfulness Code*

What it is. I have a friend who considers herself brutally honest, yet her words do not hurt at all. She has the unique skill of being able to tell the truth in a way that is easy to hear. She does not couch her comments in sweetness, nor does she shame or embarrass others. Rather, she speaks with compassion and with a true sense of caring and a desire to understand. She is also humble and takes ownership for her actions, never blaming someone else. This perfectly describes the skill of speaking mindfully.

We all know about the power of words. They can create a connection and love, and they can cause problems and even cause wars. So the practice of speaking mindfully is particularly important.

In his book The Mindfulness Code, Donald Altman describes the four components of the Buddhist concept of "right speech." This type of mindful communication must be truthful, useful and spoken at the right time. In addition, it must be kind. In other words, it cannot just be honest; it must be beneficial in some way, be spoken with affection and be conveyed at the proper moment. It must never be used as a weapon or to bring about pain or harm. At its deepest level, mindful speaking comes directly from the heart with a pure intention of connecting. As you can imagine, doing this is not easy.

How to do it. Before having a difficult conversation, run through the requirements of "right speech." Ask yourself if you can be honest and whether the information will be useful to the other person. Then figure out the right timing and select words that are kind. You can be assertive and direct, but you must avoid aggression, blaming and shaming. Speaking mindfully will not only avoid many misunderstandings and reduce potential harm, but can improve your relationships with others.

A technique I use at home and also to resolve workplace conflict is called the three Fs. Each person takes turns describing the *facts, feelings* and *future* from their perspective only. This technique incorporates mindful speech. Here is how it works.

- The first person states the *facts* from their perspective without generalizations or judgments, sticking to the precise events that happened. For example, "You promised to be home by 6:00 and now it's 6:45. I am late for my team meeting."
- Then the person describes their *feelings* and the specific impact of the other's actions. For example, "I am so frustrated because I counted on you. I am embarrassed to have to explain to my team that I am late again."
- As a final step, the same person describes what they want to happen in the *future*. This includes repairing any harm and promising to make sure it does not happen again. For example, "I would like you to call my boss and explain that you held me up. In the future I would like you to phone if you are late so I can make other arrangements."
- At this stage, the other person goes through the full three steps—stating the facts, their feelings and their wishes for the future—so they can share their perspective. By speaking mindfully and listening closely, eventually the parties come to a good understanding about what happened and can reach an agreement about what actions to take.

What to notice. You will be surprised how people respond to you when you speak in a way that includes the four components of "right speech" (truthful, useful, timed and kind). And as you practice mindful speaking, you may notice that admitting fault and being accountable for your own mistakes is enormously powerful. Indeed, admitting to mistakes often stimulates others to make the same admissions. You may find yourself being more humble and better able to show your vulnerability. Over time you may notice that under pressure, you are more able to gather your composure and reduce any knee-jerk reactions. But really what this practice is attempting to do is to bring your heart into the situation. If you choose to truly connect with the other person (and not disconnect), it's really hard to mess up.

Clarify your intentions

When we develop the habit of noticing our intentions, we have a much better compass with which to navigate our lives.
—Sharon Salzberg, *Lovingkindness*

What it is. Most of us live our lives completely unaware of our intentions. We say things and do things and then wonder why people become upset and lash out at us. We accuse others of being bothersome, irritating or offensive, not realizing that they have picked up on our subtle intent to judge them or shame them. We all use condescending tones and airs of distain, not realizing or caring that our actions may be causing harm and stress. Because our intentions are often below the surface and usually working to protect our egos, they can be dangerous to ourselves and others if we don't realize what's going on.

Behind every one of our actions is an intention, or a reason for doing something. It will be either conscious or unconscious. As we practice mindfulness, we become more aware of our intentions and thus better able to direct them in a constructive way—for the good of others or to contribute to life rather than for selfish or harmful reasons. In Buddhism, the concept of "right intention" (sometimes called "right thought") is so important that it is one of the wisdom trainings in the Noble Eightfold Path.

In their book on meditation *Five Good Minutes*, Brantley and Millstine suggest a four-part way to respond to any difficult situation.

They use the acronym LIFE which stands for Listen, Intent, Feel and Express. The four-part response entails listening deeply, being clear about your intentions, staying in touch with your feelings, and only then expressing how you feel and what you think. The most important component is the intent you bring to the conversation. If your intention is open and loving, you will find it becomes easier to express your feelings and respond in a more mindful way. Eventually, responding mindfully can become a habit.

How to do it. Take 5 minutes and just think about your typical day. Try to describe your intentions for everything you do. Why are you eating? Why are you driving? Your intentions will be varied and can range from personal to global. Are most of your intentions solely for you or for the benefit of others? Now try to set a new intention for a few of your activities. For example, you could switch your intent for eating. Rather than simply wanting to feed your body, you might want to experience the joy of chewing or taste the delightful combinations of flavors.

What to notice. As you become more aware of your hidden intentions, you will also notice more when your intentions are stopping you from enjoying life or getting in your way of having healthy relationships. You may begin to recognize when you are feeling revengeful, spiteful or jealous. You may eventually be able to stop your negative intentions from creating difficulties in your life and stop judging thoughts midstream. For example, when someone says something nasty to you, you can choose to be kind and not nasty in return. If you shift a hurtful intention and turn it around, you can produce a more enlightened response.

Practice 34

Suspend judgment

Treat people as if they were what they ought to be, and you help them become what they are capable of becoming.
—Goethe

What it is. In conflict resolution training, the two main skills we learn are listening deeply and speaking respectfully. We learn how to use our eyes and bodies to demonstrate that we care and are interested. We learn how to paraphrase and how to summarize to ensure complete understanding. And although these are useful skills, the more important skill involves a preliminary step: suspending judgment. Unless we take this initial first step, we are often in the wrong state of mind to be able to hear or respond in a way that promotes true understanding of another person's perspective. We are in essence getting in the way of ourselves.

Although judging can be a useful skill, it tends to cloud our ability to see in a fresh way. Although it helps us distinguish between safe and dangerous circumstances and keeps us from making mistakes, our judging mind is often working overtime behind the scenes—completely unconscious and often disruptive.

We go about judging almost every single thing without even noticing. Our judgments sound like this: "She is such a snob." "He is only out for himself." We judge people based on what they wear and how they look. We judge a meal before we taste it. We judge entire groups of people without even meeting them. And to make matters even worse, this judgment is often a reflection of our own self-judge.

How to do it. For a full 24-hour day, choose not to judge. Try not to judge anything or at least to suspend your judge. Do not have an opinion about a person or an event. Not your friends, spouse, teacher, workmate or children. Do not assume anything about an article in the newspaper or an advertisement on the bus. Although this is almost impossible to do, at least you will begin to notice just how much you do it. And by noticing, you can then decide if this type of judging is helpful or is preventing you from being open-minded.

What to notice. If you stop judging others, you are one step closer to freeing yourself from your own self-judgment. As you practice suspending judgment or taking a big pause before coming to a conclusion, you will see spaces open up that allow you to create connections. Although suspending judgment takes skill and prac-tice, the result is that you become curious, open-minded and free from your propensity to judge, both others and yourself.

Practice 35

Apologize and forgive

Whether we realize it or not, we pay an enormous cost for unresolved anger, grudges and grievances.
— Jeffrey Brantley and Wendy Millstine, *Five Good Minutes*

What it is. We all make mistakes and we will all continue to make mistakes over our lifetimes. We have all hurt others and have done many things "wrong." We all wish we had behaved differently. But often, rather than admitting that we were wrong, we go into hiding and harbor bad feelings for very long periods of time. Sometimes for years!

The mindful way to deal with mistakes is to accept that they happen, apologize, forgive and move on. For humans, the most difficult steps of all are apology and forgiveness, yet these steps are necessary to not just free ourselves of angst, but also to rebuild connections. When an apology is done properly, harm can be repaired almost instantaneously. Here are some examples of apologies. Try to figure out which were not effective and why.

- "SOOOOORY."
- "Sorry, but it was your fault, too."
- "Sorry, it's unfortunate it happened."
- "Sorry, it could not have been prevented."
- "Sorry, you must feel terrible."
- "I wish it hadn't happened."

- "What a stupid fool I am."
- "I won't make that mistake again."

As you can see from the above, some apologies are not only ineffective and insulting, but often cause even more harm by blaming the injured person.

Related to the apology is forgiveness. Although the idea of forgiveness is popular these days, we all struggle with forgiving. When we are hurting, it's the furthest thing from our minds. Yet forgiving is a major way to relieve stress—both forgiving ourselves and forgiving others. Forgiveness can be a miracle cure for conflict, hatred, jealousy and many other ailments. Forgiveness works to heal relationships; it releases the grip of anger and disappointment that tends to cause us all to behave badly and cling to the past. It also builds self-esteem and confidence as we take ownership for our own contribution to the conflict.

How to do it. A mindful apology is powerful, but to make it effective you must have three things: regret, acknowledgment and promise (RAP). You must show the other person you regret having caused the situation, indicate you understand how they were impacted and how they feel, and demonstrate how you will repair the situation and prevent it from happening again. Here is an example of RAP:

Regret: "I am so sorry, Maureen."
Acknowledgment: "I know you were expecting me at 6:00 p.m. and you are now late for your meeting. You must feel that I don't listen to you or respect you."
Promise: "I respect you and in future I promise I will phone when I am going to be late."

When you are making a real apology, you are not only trying to get out of trouble or off the hook, you are trying to repair the harm you caused and repair the relationship so the other party can forgive and forget. If you do not repair the relationship you may build up layers of distrust, suspicion and resentment that will surface in a later unrelated situation.

What to notice. You may notice that saying sorry in this way immediately makes the other person feel better. This is because the offended person feels heard and seen. Although apologies look simple, they are rarely easy, but the cost of not dealing with hurt feelings is extraordinarily high. Lingering bad feelings will often lurk below the surface and create tension in a perfectly healthy relationship. As well as clearing the air and rebuilding relations, apologizing is a universal way to connect as fallible human beings. It's never too late to say sorry.

Practice 36

Celebrate mistakes

No member of our global community is whole until all members
are cared for and well.
—Donald Altman, *The Mindfulness Code*

What it is. In our society we are not very tolerant of mistakes. We think they are bad and should be avoided at all costs. We indirectly tell our children that they are "bad" for doing something wrong, increasing their fear of the unknown and causing them to avoid trying new things and taking risks. Even though mistakes are a part of daily life, as parents or teachers we are in effect adding stress when we condemn them and try to prevent them. And to compound matters, when we actually do something wrong, we often berate ourselves, feeding our sense of unworthiness. We say things to ourselves like "I am hopeless" or "I am worthless." These words are very harmful.

Being mindful involves none of this torment. It involves admitting we are human and as humans we make mistakes. In fact, it means welcoming mistakes, since they are the primary way in which we learn.

You must watch a wonderful animated family movie called *Meet the Robinsons*. The main character, a teenaged orphan, is a compulsive inventor who keeps failing over and over. In one scene he invents a peanut butter and jam spreader that explodes into a complete mess. He grows up thinking no one will adopt him unless he invents something phenomenal. One day he meets a young boy who transports him to the future. There he meets a whole extended family of inventors who each not only admit to making mistakes, but actually celebrate them. In fact, their family motto is "Keep moving forward!" The orphan learns not only to accept, but also to celebrate mistakes, because that is how we grow and evolve as human beings.

How to do it. Try to celebrate your mistakes. Think of a recent mistake you made and recall what happened. Did you hide in shame and talk down to yourself, or did you openly admit to doing something wrong and come clean? One way to stop the spiral of remorse attached to making a mistake is to remind yourself that even if you did make a mistake, it does not mean you are a bad person. As a parent, I learned the technique of "separating the behavior from the child." Caregivers learn to say things like "It was bad to draw on the walls, but you are still a lovable child." We learn never to say "bad girl" or "bad boy," since it suggests the child is bad, not the action.

What to notice. It feels good to openly admit to mistakes. It feels great to say, "Yes, I completely forgot to pick up my daughter after school today, but that does not make me a bad mother." When you acknowledge your wrongs, you might feel as if a heavy weight has lifted from your shoulders. You may notice that treating yourself with compassion inspires you to be more responsible, and also triggers your desire to show compassion for others when *they* make mistakes.

Practice 37

Avoid perfectionism

Perfection is the enemy of good.
—Anonymous

What it is. Perfectionism is the belief that you have to do everything right or you will be worthless. Because of this belief, you will place enormous pressure on yourself and on others around you to succeed. Over time you will either burn out or become unhappy—finally realizing that you can never be completely perfect. Although it is important to try your best, if you expect yourself to be perfect, you are setting yourself up for failure. You will never be satisfied with yourself. Besides, perfection is boring. It is predictable, like the images of models on the covers of fashion magazines. Nothing stands out.

From the time they are little, we also tell our children to be perfect. We tell them to be at the top of their class, play on several sports teams and be concert musicians. Many kids feel they must do everything perfectly. Yet the truth is that there is no such thing as perfection, and as a result, you will always fail. Even Olympians have bad days. The pursuit of perfectionism often lasts a lifetime and can be quite destructive, so try these practices to avoid and overcome it.

How to do it. The first way to avoid perfectionism is to simply notice it in yourself. Do you have high expectations of yourself at home, school or work? Did your parents have high expectations of you? Do you think you will be rejected if you are not exceptional? In what ways does your perfectionism work for you? How is it harming you? The main way to combat perfectionism is through self-love and self-compassion. You can say things to yourself like the following:

- I am "perfect" just the way I am.
- I am lovable and valuable as a human being.
- I am learning and growing as best I can.
- I like myself just as I am and accept my flaws.
- I do not need to be perfect.
- I forgive myself when I make mistakes.
- I can go easy on myself.

What to notice. Like many of us, you may not have even realized that you were striving for perfection. You might not have noticed the heavy toll of your high standards. You also may not have noticed how your own personal standards are impacting those you love. As you notice, you will free yourself psychologically and come to understand that perfectionism is not only impossible, but also sucks the joy out of life and hurts relationships.

Practice 38

Practice optimism

Habitual energy patterns block us from the richness of life, moment by moment, but you don't have to remain stuck in these patterns. There is another way beyond one of inattention, contraction and reactivity.
—Jeffrey Brantley and Wendy Millstine, *Five Good Minutes*

What it is. Martin Seligman, author of the books *Learned Optimism* and *Authentic Happiness*, stressed the importance of optimism. In his research, he found out that those people who are optimistic are happier and live longer. They appreciate life and tend to make the best out of what they have. Pessimists, on the other hand, tend to see the glass as half empty and look at things from a negative perspective.

Seligman noticed that the difference between optimists and pessimists was in how they viewed bad things that happened to them. Optimists thought that the bad thing was temporary and rare, while pessimists thought the event was permanent or frequent. In other words, optimists felt that although bad things happen, they rarely occur, and when they do, they tend not to last very long.

Since the only difference was in how they thought, Seligman surmised that optimism could be learned. In other words, we can live less stressful lives and be happier by simply learning how to see things from a more positive perspective. Like mindfulness, we watch our thinking and notice the harm it is causing. Then we show ourselves compassion as we learn how to shift pessimism to a more constructive habit.

How to do it. Seligman teaches a specific way to become more optimistic. The key to disputing your own pessimistic thoughts is to first notice them and then to treat them as if they were being spoken out loud by another person whose aim in life is to make you miserable.

Here is Seligman's five-step model. By becoming mindful of your pessimistic thoughts, you can counteract them by using this ABCDE model.

A Notice the *adversity* or event that gives rise to the pessimistic thought.
B Pay attention to the *beliefs* you automatically have when it happens.
C Look at the usual *consequences* or your reactions to what happened.
D Try to *dispute* your belief, usually by using evidence, logic or affirmations.
E Notice the *energization* that occurs (e.g., feeling lighter and more full of life).

Here is an example. Let's say a friend does not call (*adversity*), so you think she no longer likes you (*belief*). You ignore her the next day (*consequences*). When you learn she was at the hospital with her sick father, you are able to *dispute* your belief and as a result feel much better (*energization*). Notice these are all just thoughts, nothing more.

As you can see, by effectively disputing your beliefs, you can change your reaction from dejection to calm or being harmful to being positive.

What to notice. By going through each of the five steps, you can untangle where you might be getting stuck and causing yourself more angst. For example, if your girlfriend does not call, you might freak out initially but then notice that your thoughts were quite distorted. This is called "catastrophizing," or exaggerating the possible harm from a relatively minor event. The most difficult step for all of us is disputing our belief. This is because our beliefs are so deeply engrained and hidden in our subconscious. Yet the practice of being mindful of these beliefs is extraordinarily powerful at freeing us from them.

Notice your triggers

The first and most important step is to stop. Whenever you feel triggered just stop. Pausing at the outset of a trigger is a very powerful and important skill. Do not react for just one moment. This moment is known as the sacred pause.
—Chade-Meng Tan, *Search Inside Yourself*

What it is. We all have triggers. These are situations that cause us to overreact or shut down emotionally. At a party someone might mention your weight, and you immediately become overwhelmed with a sense of shame or embarrassment. Your teacher or boss might tell you to keep your voice down and you will feel like crying, recalling the personal insults or rejections you might have suffered as a child. By being more mindful, you can not only learn more about your specific triggers, but also notice when you get hooked and how you spiral down. Eventually, you can learn how to antici-pate your triggers and develop skills to both temper their impact and help you develop a more mindful response.

How to do it. Recall the last time you were triggered and try to recall three things: first, the impact on your body; second, your feelings or emotions; and third, your thoughts. For example, you may have no-ticed your breathing becoming shallow, your heart rate increasing, your jaw clenching or a sense of dread in the pit of your stomach.

Next notice your emotions, such as irritation, anger, frustration or hurt. Do you feel the urge to scream or to hide? Finally notice your thoughts. Are you feeling injured, slighted, rejected or insulted? Notice how your feelings are directly related to your thoughts and vice versa. Now that you are removed from the event, and in a calm state of mind, your thinking may be different. This is why it's often best to wait a while before responding when highly agitated. In an overwhelmed state, we can cause both ourselves and others harm.

What to notice. If you practice being mindful around your triggers, you will be able to slow your response and will find it easier to handle difficult situations. You may look back and wonder why past triggers impacted you so powerfully, and you may have a deeper understanding about them and their root causes. The key is not to stop feeling or to reject your emotions, but rather to feel them without becoming completely overwhelmed.

Question productivity and time

*A thoroughly and good relationship with ourselves results in be-
ing still, which doesn't mean we don't run and jump and dance
about.... It means there is no compulsiveness. We don't over-
work, overeat, over smoke, over seduce. In short, we begin to
stop causing harm.*

—Pema Chödrön, *Start Where You Are*

What it is. In our culture, we worship productivity. We think the only
things worthwhile are those that produce some measurable, tangi-
ble and immediate result. Many of us measure our self-worth based
on what we produce. This causes us to work furiously toward some
goal without really ever being in the present moment. We are too
busy on our way to somewhere else, and when we arrive, we simply
set another goal and head off toward it right away.

In her book *Simple Days*, Marlene Schiwy reminds us that that
productivity does not equal meaning and that there is no use
streamlining our work and saving precious minutes and hours if we
lack a purpose and meaning in our lives. As she says, "We stream-
line the activities of the day for the greatest efficiency, getting rid of
the small human exchanges that give our lives warmth and texture.
Then we rush off at night to a course on mindfulness or a workshop

on walking meditation or building relationships, desperate to re-claim—for a hefty fee—what we have devalued and thrown way."

There is a great story about two pilots flying across the Atlantic Ocean. The co-pilot turns to the pilot and says, "I have some good news and some bad news." When the pilot asks for the good news first, the co-pilot replies, "The good news is that we are flying faster and straighter than we ever have before. This plane is working at its highest level of efficiency and effectiveness." Then he pauses, "The bad news, however, is that we are completely and utterly lost."

In her book *How to Train a Wild Elephant*, Jan Chozen Bays says, "If I did not produce anything today; if I did not write a book, give a speech, bake bread, earn money, sell something, buy something, get a good grade on a test, or find my soul mate, then my day was just wasted and I'm a failure. We give ourselves no credit for taking 'being'-time for just being in the present. 'Waiting' is then a source of frustration. Think of the things I could have been getting done." This practice counteracts the Western approach to time.

How to do it. We all have very odd ideas about time and productivi-ty. We can uncover these ideas through the use of metaphors, as demonstrated by Marlene Schiwy. Before looking at Schiwy's list below, brainstorm some of the metaphors or phrases that you use when talking about time. For example, "Time is money," or "I have no time." Review your list and notice how the phrases reflect your underlying assumptions about time and productivity. Also notice how these assumptions contribute to your stress.

Here are some of Marlene's examples: "Spending time, investing time, saving time, borrowing time, beating time, hoarding time, defying time, managing time, needing time, lacking time, squandering time, buying time, wasting time, gaining time, passing time, using time, tak-ing time, killing time, running out of time, being out of time."

What to notice. The Western notion of time causes us all to become crazed workaholics. We feel like we are on an endless treadmill, never having enough time. Since we think there is never enough time, we think we must maximize it and in our complete haste we have very little room for fun, relaxation, joy or comfort. If we are not doing something productive, we feel our time is wasted. This is sad. As Schiwy says, "We want to control time and squeeze every ounce of life from it, and yet tragically, in the process we rob ourselves of the present which is the only time we really ever have."

Chapter 5

Your Life

Practice 41

Do mindful art

We're fools whether we dance or not, so we might as well dance.
—Japanese proverb

What it is. I attended an art therapy class last year and it completely surprised me. Each day we used a different medium, like clay or paints or poetry, to help us explore deeper feelings and thoughts. The class was fun and also helped provide significant insights and inner peace.

In her book *The Soul's Palette*, Cathy Malchiodi shows how art can help heal and even uncover hidden health issues. By noticing the images in other pieces of art or in producing our own art, we gain insight and understanding. She says, "Images are the loving messengers from the soul's palette and, as seen here, have the potential to remind us to take care of ourselves and to bring wellness and wholeness to both the body and the soul."

How to do it. Set aside one hour and find a blank piece of letter-size paper and some old magazines. Flip through the magazine pages paying complete attention to the colors and shapes that are pleasing to you. Also notice the images that you find odd or distasteful. Cut and paste bits and pieces and put them in a pile. Then spread them all over the floor and sit back and look at them. Move them around and notice any sensations or feelings that arise. Select the ones that "speak to you" and put aside the rest. Look at them from every angle and place them onto the blank piece of paper in a way that feels calm, comforting and soothing. You may want to do some self-exploration by asking yourself questions like "What are these colors, shapes and images saying to me now?" and "How does it feel now?" Then glue them in place. Add other colors and shapes if you wish. Keep it handy to look at later and see if it induces a sense of calm.

What to notice. When you engage in art or art therapy, a few things happen. Although you might feel stuck initially, if you truly step into the practice, you will be begin to feel free and not so worried about your artistic results. By working with your hands and with shapes, you inadvertently tap your creativity and intuition and allow tensions to release without effort. As you relax into the art, you may find you gain insight in a curious and nonjudgmental way.

Practice 42

Try a labyrinth or mandala

What lies behind us and what lies before us are tiny matters
compared to what lies within us.
—Henry Stanley Haskins, *Meditations in Wall Street*

What it is. In my side yard, I built a large labyrinth using hundreds of rocks from my garden. When people walk by they think it is maze, not realizing that it is an ancient tool for meditation and mindfulness. One summer my daughters and I created block prints of labyrinths and printed hundreds up on small pieces of cloth as portable "finger labyrinths" that we could carry with us.

The labyrinth (and the mandala—see below) are contemplation or meditation tools that help with concentration and focus and also induce a calm, meditative state. The labyrinth is a maze-like shape often set within a circle that has no branches and gives you no choices. Originating in ancient times, labyrinths are often made of stone and can be found all over the world; many have deep spiritual significance. The most famous labyrinth is in the Chartres Cathedral in France, a "Pilgrim Labyrinth" carved into its floor. As a walking meditation tool, the pathway is designed to confuse and refocus the person walking so they can clear their mind. Like a journey to the center that winds through twists and turns, in walking the labyrinth you move from confusion to understanding.

A mandala is also a meditation tool. It is an image or drawing that is created in the shape of a circle. The shape represents the relationship between the outer world (the circle) and the inner world (the mind). The geometric shapes that form are said to be useful in understanding divine wisdom and enlightenment. Carl Jung thought the mandala was a symbol that represented the total personality or the "Self." Joan Kellogg, the art therapist who spent most of her life studying the mandala, called it the "Great Round." As Cathy Malchiodi says, self-created mandalas are reflections of our inner selves and are symbolic of our potential for change and transformation.

How to do it. Find a labyrinth in a church, park or on paper or fabric. Stand still at the opening, make a request for clarity on anything, and then simply walk slowly. When you get to the center, stop and relax. Open yourself to wisdom, and then begin your journey back. When you have completed your walk, give thanks. Find a mandala in a book or online and simply look at it. As you gaze, you may be able to move your mind from chaos (the outer circle) to the still point in the middle.

What to notice. Even when you just look at them, the mandala and the labyrinth often evoke a sense of peace and connectedness. As in meditation, while drawing a mandala or walking a labyrinth, various thoughts might show up and fade away. Many people find it easy to use these tools to cause their minds to stay quiet so inner wisdom can surface.

Practice 43

Create a sacred space

*In the attitude of silence, the soul finds the path in a clearer light,
and what is elusive and deceptive resolves itself into crystal
clearness.*
—Gandhi

What it is. Although you can be mindful anywhere, it's helpful when establishing a practice to set aside a specific space in which to sit. You may want to create a shrine or altar as a focal point and a reminder of your commitment to always remain mindful. As in a church, a synagogue or other place of worship, this space provides a quiet place of solitude to make it easier to focus your attention when meditating.

How to do it. Set aside a room or a small area or corner within a room. You can add a collection of things you love or you can add an altar. Some people like to include symbols of the four elements: earth, fire, water and air. You could collect, for example, a crystal, a candle, a bowl of water, and some incense. For sound you could listen to prerecorded meditations, quiet music or chanting. It's fun to mix it up periodically, perhaps with the change of the seasons.

What to notice. With a designated space for your mindfulness practice, you will find yourself sitting still more often, both in the space and outside it. You will eventually feel a special type of energy in that space that will enhance your ability to meditate, visualize or simply relax.

Practice 44

Dance

*Those who danced were thought to be quite insane by those
who could not hear the music.*
—Angela Monet

What it is. A large part of mindfulness involves reconnecting to our bodies, learning about them and activating them. In our society we tend to think of our bodies as things that need to be fed and exercised, like an industrial machine. We do not see them as creative and magnificent biological, neurological and energetic organisms that are expanding as we think, as we feel, as we interact with others and as we move them in dance and exercise.

Ken Robinson, a brilliant educator, became famous for his TED Talk on the failings of education. He helped viewers see how our North American and British entire education systems, from kindergarten to grade 12, were designed to educate only the head. The rest of the body was just carried along. As a result, most public schools today do not teach a significant amount of music, art or dance. And yet we know that the ability to do these things directly impacts our ability to learn all the other subjects. Sadly, not only do we rarely teach body movement or dance, our children come to think of the body as separate from their minds. Those who do practice dance know the power of moving the muscles, joints and bones for their well-being.

How to do it. Sign up for a body movement course such as qigong, yoga, tai chi or Nia. These practices are designed to allow your body to move in natural and unforced ways.

What to notice. Not only do you gain flexibility, but you often feel an energetic release when you make body movement a regular part of your life. Some believe that chi or life energy can get blocked in your muscles and joints, and you must move them to allow it to move more freely.

Practice 45

Never judge a book
by its cover

What it is. This Zen tale teaches us not to assume too much and to keep an open mind.

How to do it. Read this poem aloud.

Perhaps (a Zen tale)

Once upon a time there lived an old farmer who had worked his crops for many years. He had only one son and one horse. His wife had passed on many years ago.

One day his only horse ran away. Upon hearing the news, his neighbors came to visit. With sympathetic voices they said: "Such bad luck. Now what will you use to plow your fields? Such terrible luck!" At the farmer simply replied, "Perhaps."

The next morning the farmer's horse returned, bringing with it three other wild horses. Upon hearing the great news, the neighbors came back to visit and exclaimed: "How wonderful for you. So many horses. Such riches. Such wonderful luck!" And the old man replied, "Perhaps."

The following day, the farmer's only son was trying to tame one of the wild horses. He was thrown off and broke his leg. When the neighbors heard, they came running over. They said: "Such misfortune. You will not have your son to help you with your crops. You will need to tend to him. This is such back luck for you!" And in response the farmer said, "Perhaps."

The day after that, military officials came to the village to draft young men into the army. Seeing that the farmer's son's leg was broken, they passed him by. The neighbors later came by to offer the farmer congratulations at being able to save his son from the possibility of dying at war. They said "Such good luck!" And to this, the farmer replied, "Perhaps."

What to notice. I hope you smiled at the end of this tale. It's a beautiful example of how quick we are to judge things as good or bad, yet our assumptions rarely come true. After reading this, you should have a sense of opportunity or anticipation that anything could happen. You never know.

Practice 46

Live life with joy

If the mind is not contrived, it is spontaneously blissful, just as water, when not agitated, is by nature transparent and clear.
—Traditional Tibetan saying

What it is. We often live life as if it is one big chore. We think we are just doing our job when we go to school or to work. But in reality we are living life in a constant relationship with everything. We are embracing, interacting and unfolding with everything. Life is actually interacting with us!

How to do it. Read this poem to begin to understand how you can better let life live through you. This is a popular Buddhist tale that celebrates simply living life without judging each event as good or bad. Life is about embracing it all.

Hokusai says
by Roger Keyes

Hokusai says look carefully.
He says pay attention, notice.
He says keep looking, stay curious.
He says there is no end to seeing.

He says look forward to getting old.
He says keep changing,
you just get more who you really are.
He says get stuck, accept it, repeat yourself
as long as it's interesting.

He says keep doing what you love.

He says keep praying.

He says every one of us is a child,
every one of us is ancient,
every one of us has a body.
He says every one of us is frightened.
He says every one of us has to find
a way to live with fear.

He says everything is alive—
shells, buildings, people, fish,
mountains, trees. Wood is alive.
Water is alive.

Everything has its own life.

Everything lives inside us.

He says live with the world inside you.

He says it doesn't matter if you draw,
or write books. It doesn't matter
if you saw wood, or catch fish.
It doesn't matter if you sit at home
and stare at the ants on your veranda
or the shadows of the trees
and grasses in your garden.

It matters that you care.

It matters that you feel.

It matters that you notice.

It matters that life lives through you.

Contentment is life living through you.
Joy is life living through you.
Satisfaction and strength
is life living through you.
Peace is life living through you.
He says don't be afraid.
Don't be afraid.

Love, feel, let life take you by the hand.

Let life live through you.

What to notice. After reading this poem, you should feel at peace and more in the flow of life. It may inspire you to see things in a fresh and different way. Read it often and you will experience a different impact each time.

Embrace all of life

What it is. As humans, we are constantly running away from pain. We look at bad things that happen as attacks on us. As a result, we push away these bad things and try to avoid them. In doing so, we cause ourselves more suffering. The mindful way is to embrace everything in life, good, bad and in between.

What to do. Read this poem to begin to understand how you can embrace everything that comes your way. This is a poem that teaches us to be open to all.

The guest house
by Jalaluddin Rumi
(translation by Coleman Barks)

This being human is a guest house.
Every morning a new arrival.

A joy, a depression, a meanness,
some momentary awareness comes
as an unexpected visitor.

Welcome and entertain them all!
Even if they are a crowd of sorrows,

who violently sweep your house
empty of its furniture,
still, treat each guest honorably.
He may be clearing you out
for some new delight.

The dark thought, the shame, the malice
meet them at the door laughing and invite them in.

Be grateful for whatever comes
because each has been sent
as a guide from beyond.

What to notice. After reading this poem, you should feel more able to deal with the ups and downs of life. It may motivate you to look at life events in a more open-minded way.

Practice 48

Feast on life

What it is. This is one of my favorite poems, by a friend of mine.

How to do it. Read this poem to help you embrace all your joys and your sorrows. This is a poem that teaches us to be open to all.

Feast
by Rachel Rose

The table is set with stars. Come to the table.
Put away your anger and your guitar.
The apples are baking. Tallow drips from candles.

Nothing can hold back death. Come to the table.
Set your burnt spoon aside in a difficult drawer.
Wipe the sin from your mouth. Come as soon as you're able.

The wheat's in the barn and the barge. The babe's in the cradle.
The history that led to the railway cars
is a trunk you can leave at the dock. Unbridle, unsaddle

the dappled horse in your greathearted fable
the horse that you rode to the battle, and then to the wars.
The salmon's been pulled from the sea, and served with its shadow.

Come to the table, beloved, the three-legged table,
for you are the bell jar's hammer, the broken-down door.
What's crooked finds balance on matchbooks and elbows.

O prodigal child. O sage of the bluegrass piano!
The buckets catch buckshot that falls from a bonfire of stars.
You were stabbed in both hands by the bees that you robbed in the
    grotto.
We'll serve honey in moon-mist. We'll capture tornadoes in jars.
    Come to the table.

What to notice. This poem reminds us that there is no such thing
as the perfect pain-free life. It is not something to aim for. After
reading this poem, you may feel more accepting of all that life
throws at you. We can feast on all of life!

(Originally published in *Marry & Burn*, 2015 (Harbour Publishing, Canada)

Accept your journey

What it is. This is a very funny but true poem about how we learn the hard way—through trial and error, becoming slowly wiser each day.

How to do it. Read this poem to help you accept that you are an ever-growing human being, continually making mistakes. And this is okay.

Autobiography in five short chapters
by Portia Nelson

Chapter One
I walk down the street.
　There is a deep hole in the sidewalk.
　I fall in.
　I am lost.... I am helpless.
　　It isn't my fault.
It takes forever to find a way out.

Chapter Two
I walk down the same street.
　There is a deep hole in the sidewalk.
　I pretend I don't see it.

I fall in again.
I can't believe I am in the same place.
     But, it isn't my fault.
It still takes me a long time to get out.

Chapter Three

I walk down the same street.
     There is a deep hole in the sidewalk.
     I see it is there.
     I still fall in...It's a habit...but,
     my eyes are open.
     I know where I am.
It is *my* fault.
I get out immediately.

Chapter Four

I walk down the same street.
     There is a deep hole in the sidewalk.
     I walk around it.

Chapter Five

I walk down another street.

What to notice. This poem reminds us that we learn slowly and there is no way to prevent falling down and getting up. This is the story of entire lives. It is useful to meditate on the times we have fallen down and the lessons we learn.

Practice 50

Accept yourself completely

What it is. I used to read this prayer almost every day. It's a great tool for developing self-love and self-compassion and embracing the parts of our self that we might not be particularly fond of.

How to do it. Read this poem to help you accept yourself completely.

Daily prayer of acceptance
by Lise Storgaard

I accept myself completely.
I accept my strengths and my weaknesses, my gifts and my short-
    comings.
I accept myself completely as a human being.
I accept that I am here to learn and grow, and
I accept that I am learning and growing.
I accept the personality I've developed, and
I accept my power to heal and change.

I accept myself without condition or reservation.
I accept that the core of my being is goodness and that my essence
    is love, and
I accept that I sometimes forget that.

I accept myself completely, and in this acceptance I find an ever-
     deepening inner strength.
From this place of strength, I accept my life fully and
I open to the lessons it offers me each day.

I accept that within my mind are both fear and love, and
I accept my power to choose which I will experience as real.
I recognize that I experience only the results of my own choices.

I accept the times that I choose fear as part of my learning and
     healing process, and
I accept that I have the potential and power in any moment to
     choose love instead.

I accept mistakes as a part of growth,
I am willing to forgive myself and give myself another chance.
I accept that my life is the expression of my thought, and
I commit myself to aligning my thoughts more and more each day
     with the thought of Love.
I accept that I am an expression of this Love.
I am Love's hands, voice and heart on Earth.

I accept my own life as a blessing and a gift.
My heart is open to receive, and I am deeply grateful.
May I always share the gifts that I receive fully, freely, and joyfully.
I accept all that I was, all that I am, and all that I choose to become.

What to notice. This poem is such a beautiful reminder to accept absolutely everything. It shows that by acceptance we can let go of trying to struggle to make everything "perfect" and that there is no such thing as perfection.

Conclusion

The practice of mindfulness has changed my life completely. Although it took me a long time to integrate the practices into my daily life, it has been well worth the effort. I urge you to play with the practices and create your own. Share them with others and simply see what shows up. And of course enjoy the journey.

It's good to have an end to journey toward; but it is the journey that matters in the end.
—Ursula LeGuin

Resources

Books

Altman, Donald. *The Mindfulness Code: Keys to Overcoming Stress, Anxiety, Fear and Unhappiness*. New World Library, 2010.

Brach, Tara. *Radical Acceptance: Embracing Your Life with the Heart of a Buddha*. Bantam, 2003.

Brantley, Jeffrey, and Wendy Millstine. *Five Good Minutes: 100 Morning Practices to Help You Stay Calm and Focused All Day*. New Harbinger, 2005.

Chödrön, Pema. *Start Where You Are: A Guide to Compassionate Living*. Shambhala, 2001.

Chozen Bays, Jan. *How to Train a Wild Elephant: And Other Adventures in Mindfulness*. Shambhala, 2011.

Dalai Lama and Paul Ekman. *Emotional Awareness: Overcoming the Obstacles to Psychological Balance and Compassion*. Holt, 2009.

Digh, Patti. *Life Is a Verb: 37 Days to Wake Up, Be Mindful, and Live Intentionally*. Skirt!, 2008.

Epstein, Mark. *Thoughts Without a Thinker: Psychotherapy from a Buddhist Perspective*. Basic Books, 1995.

———. *Going to Pieces Without Falling Apart: A Buddhist Perspective on Wholeness*. Broadway Books, 1998.

Fitzgerald, Maureen F. *Mission Possible: Creating a Mission for Work and Life*. Quinn Publishing, 2003.

Fischer, Norman. *Opening to You: Zen-Inspired Translations of the Psalms*. Penguin Books, 2003.

Gibran, Kahlil. *The Prophet*. Knopf, 1973.

Goldstein, Joseph. *Insight Meditation: The Practice of Freedom*. Shambhala, 2003.

Goleman, Daniel. *Emotional intelligence: Why It Can Matter More Than IQ*. Bantam Books, 1995. 10th anniversary edition, 2005.

———. *Social Intelligence: The New Science of Human Relationships*. Bantam Books, 2006.

Gunaratana, Bhante. *Mindfulness in Plain English*. Wisdom Publications, 1992. 20th anniversary edition, 2011.

Hope, Jane. *The Meditation Year*. Storey Publishing, 2001.

Kabat-Zinn, Jon. *Full Catastrophe Living: Using the Wisdom of Your Mind to Face Stress, Pain, and Illness*. Delta, 1990. Revised and updated edition, Bantam, 2013.

———. *Wherever You Go, There You Are: Mindfulness in Everyday Life*. Hyperion, 1994.

———. *Coming to Our Senses: Healing Ourselves and the World Through Mindfulness*. Hyperion, 2005.

Kornfield, Jack. *A Path with Heart: A Guide Through the Perils and Promises of Spiritual Life*. Bantam Books, 1993.

———. *After the Ecstasy, the Laundry: How the Heart Grows Wise on the Spiritual Path*. Bantam Books, 2000.

Malchiodi, Cathy. *The Soul's Palette: Drawing on Art's Powers for Health and Well-Being*. Shambhala, 2012.

Moffitt, Phillip. *Dancing with Life: Buddhist Insights for Finding Meaning and Joy in the Face of Suffering*. Rodale, 2008.

Nelson, Portia. *There's a Hole in My Sidewalk: The Romance of Self-Discovery*. Beyond Words Publishing, 1993. 35th anniversary edition, Simon & Schuster, 2012.

Roland, Paul. *How to Meditate: An Illustrated Guide to Calming the Mind and Relaxing the Body*. Ulysses Press, 2000.

Rosenberg, Marshall. *Nonviolent Communication: A Language of Life*. Puddle Dancer Press, 2003.

Salzberg, Sharon. *Lovingkindness: The Revolutionary Art of Happiness*. Shambhala Classics, 2002.

Salzman, Amy. *A Still Quiet Place: A Mindfulness Program for Teaching Children and Adolescents to Ease Stress and Difficult Emotions*. New Harbinger Publications, 2014.

Schiwy, Marlene. *Simple Days: A Journal on What Really Matters*. Sorin Books, 2002.

Seligman, Martin. *Learned Optimism: How to Change Your Mind and Your Life*. Vintage, 2006. Reprint edition.

———. *Authentic Happiness: Using the New Positive Psychology to Realize Your Potential for Lasting Fulfillment*. Atria Books, 2004.

Siegel, Daniel. *The Mindful Brain: Reflection and Attunement in the Cultivation of Well-Being*. Norton, 2007.

———. *Mindsight: The New Science of Personal Transformation*. Bantam Books, 2010.

Stahl, Bob, and Elisha Goldstein. *A Mindfulness-Based Stress Reduction Workbook*. New Harbinger Publications, 2010.

Tan, Chade-Meng. *Search Inside Yourself: The Unexpected Path to Achieving Success, Happiness (and World Peace)*. Harper One, 2014.

Tart, Charles T. *Living the Mindful Life: A Handbook for Living in the Present Moment*. Shambhala, 1994.

Tolle, Eckhart. *The Power of Now: A Guide to Spiritual Enlightenment*. Namaste, 2004.

Websites and videos

Authentic Happiness. Positive Psychology Center, University of Pennsylvania. Martin E.P. Seligman is the center's director and a professor of psychology at Penn. www.authentichappiness.org

Center for Mindfulness in Medicine, Health Care, and Society. University of Massachusetts Medical School. Home to the Mindfulness-Based Stress Reduction (MBSR) program. www.umassmed.edu/cfm

Ensler, Eve. "I Am an Emotional Creature" [YouTube video]. www.youtube.com/watch?v=alOm_kpYIiw

Hawn, Goldie [Founder]. Hawn Foundation, which originated the MindUP training program for educators and children. www.thehawnfoundation.org

Mindfulness-Based Cognitive Therapy (MBCT) website developed by Zindel Segal, Mark Williams and John Teasdale. http://mbct.com

Robinson, Ken [Author/educator]. TED Talks that challenge the way
we're educating our children. www.ted.com/speakers/sir_ken_ robinson

About the Author

Maureen F. Fitzgerald, PhD is a change agent, author and recovering lawyer. Having written several books and hundreds of blogs she is a "maven on a mission" to open minds and hearts. She practiced law for over 20 years and is the founder of Centerpoint Media. Her mission is to open minds and hearts through her writing and speaking – to make the world a better place.

Maureen is author of 12 books, including *Occupy Women, Lean Out* and *Invite the Bully to Tea*. She has a business degree from the University of Alberta, a law degree from the University of Western Ontario, a master's degree in law with distinction from the London School of Economics and a doctorate degree from the University of British Columbia.

In her former career, Maureen was a labor lawyer, a policy lawyer and a mediator. She was also a professor of law at two universities and has written many articles, both academic and practical.

Maureen speaks at retreats, conferences, professional association events, women's organizations, corporate training, non-profit events and conventions. Always a leader of both people and ideas. Her motto is: Sharing the right ideas at the right time can change the world. You can find her at *www.MaureenFitzgerald.com*.

Also by the Author

Lean Out: Shatter the Glass Ceiling to Success, Happiness and Work-life Balance

Motherhood Is Madness: Break the Chains to Happiness as a Mother and Wife

Occupy Women: A Manifesto for Success, Happiness and Freedom in a World Run by Men

If Not Now, When? Create a Life and Career of Purpose with a Powerful Vision, a Mission Statement and Measurable Goals

A Woman's Circle: Create a Peer Mentoring Group for Advice, Networking, Support and Connection

Invite the Bully to Tea: End Harassment, Bullying and Dysfunction Forever with a Simple Yet Radical New Approach

Hiring, Managing and Keeping the Best: The Complete Canadian Guide for Employers, With Monica Beauregard

So You Think You Need a Lawyer: How to Screen, Hire, Manage or Fire a Lawyer

Legal Problem Solving: Reasoning, Research and Writing. (7th ed.) Lexis/Nexis

Made in the USA
Charleston, SC
11 January 2016